Air Strike

Other Publications:

HOW THINGS WORK
WINGS OF WAR
CREATIVE EVERYDAY COOKING
COLLECTOR'S LIBRARY OF THE UNKNOWN
CLASSICS OF WORLD WAR II
TIME-LIFE LIBRARY OF CURIOUS AND UNUSUAL FACTS
AMERICAN COUNTRY
VOYAGE THROUGH THE UNIVERSE
THE THIRD REICH
THE TIME-LIFE GARDENER'S GUIDE
MYSTERIES OF THE UNKNOWN
TIME FRAME
FIX IT YOURSELF
FITNESS, HEALTH & NUTRITION
SUCCESSFUL PARENTING
HEALTHY HOME COOKING
UNDERSTANDING COMPUTERS
LIBRARY OF NATIONS
THE ENCHANTED WORLD
THE KODAK LIBRARY OF CREATIVE PHOTOGRAPHY
GREAT MEALS IN MINUTES
THE CIVIL WAR
PLANET EARTH
COLLECTOR'S LIBRARY OF THE CIVIL WAR
THE EPIC OF FLIGHT
THE GOOD COOK
WORLD WAR II
HOME REPAIR AND IMPROVEMENT
THE OLD WEST

For information on and a full description of
any of the Time-Life Books series listed above,
please call 1-800-621-7026 or write:
Reader Information
Time-Life Customer Service
P.O. Box C-32068
Richmond, Virginia 23261-2068

THE
NEW
FACE
OF
WAR

Air Strike

BY THE EDITORS OF
TIME-LIFE BOOKS, ALEXANDRIA, VIRGINIA

CONSULTANTS

LIEUTENANT COLONEL NELSON L. BEARD, a U.S. Air Force fighter pilot, has more than 2,000 hours' flying time in F-4 Phantoms. In 1983 he was awarded Egyptian Air Force wings while flying F-4s in Cairo. He has also flown extensively in Europe and the Pacific as well as the Middle East.

BRIAN COOPER is Director of Business Development for C^3I (Command, Control, Communications and Intelligence) Systems at Fairchild Defense in Germantown, Maryland. He has more than twenty years' experience in advanced digital systems design.

MAJOR LINCOLN QUIGLEY, an F-4 Phantom II fighter pilot, has participated in ten Red Flag exercises. He has flown with or against the naval and air arms of twelve nations, accumulating over 3,100 hours' flying time in various models of the Phantom.

COLONEL T. C. SKANCHY, recently retired from the U.S. Air Force, commanded a fighter wing and the F-15 Division, Fighter Weapons School, at Nellis Air Force Base, Nevada. He also served there as the vice commander of Red Flag, the Air Force's combined air operations training program.

CONTENTS

1

And Bombs Fell on Baghdad

Photographed through night-vision equipment, an F-117A stealth fighter inches toward a tanker's refueling boom *(top)* to gas up en route to bomb Baghdad during Operation Desert Wind. To help the boom operator connect with the refueling receptacle, it is illuminated from a bright light that the pilot douses, along with position lights on the fuselage and wing tips, before resuming his flight toward the target.

As soon as Eric Rankin heard the knock at the door, just after midnight on Thursday, January 17, 1991, he knew something was amiss. A television reporter with the Canadian Broadcasting Corporation, Rankin had come to Baghdad five days earlier to make a documentary about Iraq's preparations for war—something that he, like many of the other Western journalists staying at the Rashid Hotel, figured would not break out for another two or three days. Opening the door, he found a correspondent from CBS standing in the hallway. The Pentagon, said the American, had just sent his network a coded message containing a prearranged warning: Iraq would be attacked in two or three hours.

Until that moment, Rankin had assumed that he would be long gone before any bombs fell. In fact, he was scheduled to fly out of the country the next morning. But now he was unsure. If an attack did come, he thought, it would start in the air, and no airliner would be allowed to depart Saddam International Airport. If the overland route to Jordan was closed at the same time, he would be stranded. Worse, though, was the realization that the capital city—his home for another night—would be a likely target. Not knowing exactly what to expect in an air raid, he and his crew set up a camera near the window in their ninth-floor room and spent the next two and a half hours waiting and watching.

At 2:32 a.m., Rankin saw a single red tracer ascend from the horizon. Then other antiaircraft artillery, louder than the first, directed its fire into less distant sections of the moonless sky. Seconds later, still more guns joined in the frenzied chorus, and bright flashes starkly illuminated the jumble of domes, monuments, and high-rise apartment buildings in the capital. "It was as if the Iraqis had antiaircraft guns scattered every half-block or so throughout the city," Rankin said. "From horizon to horizon, there was nothing but red tracer bullets arching up into the sky."

One of the batteries was positioned only a hundred yards from the Rashid, on top of a building about nine stories tall. From his window, Rankin could watch the Iraqi gunners as they swung their cannons from side to side, spraying tracers in shimmering S-shaped patterns. "It was hypnotizing; it was beautiful to watch," Rankin said, "but the sound was what was unbelievable. The antiaircraft guns. When they opened up, the sound would literally go right through you. It would make you grit your teeth."

As the gunners pounded away, Rankin looked in vain for attacking aircraft. Sparkling blue-white bursts of flak flashed overhead, and explosions rumbled in the distance, but no jet planes, no incoming missiles could be seen or heard. The Iraqis seemed to be firing at an empty sky. "I really don't think they knew what they were shooting at," Rankin said. "They were just firing everything they had into the sky, hoping to hit something." After twenty minutes, the guns fell silent, and as dogs across Baghdad bayed, a lull settled over the capital.

Rankin had become a witness to war. Five and a half months after Iraq had invaded its wealthy neighbor Kuwait, a multinational coalition led by the United States had begun the campaign to drive the occupiers out. The action followed a trade embargo that had been imposed by the United Nations Security Council on Iraq immediately after the invasion in an effort to resolve the impasse without bloodshed. But as time passed and diplomacy faltered, Saddam Hussein, Iraq's dictator, only became more intransigent. In October, he threatened to fire missiles at Israel if his 400,000-man army in Kuwait was attacked. And in November, instead of withdrawing the force, he buttressed it with a quarter-million more soldiers. By the end of the month, patience with the sanctions had waned, and the Security Council issued an ultimatum: If Iraq did not withdraw by 8:00 a.m. on January 16, Baghdad time, the coalition would be authorized to liberate Kuwait by force.

On the day of the deadline, Rankin had observed few indications that the city was preparing for war. Some well-off Baghdadis, fearing the worst, had checked into the Rashid Hotel; they intended to take refuge, if necessary, in its massive underground bomb shelter. Others had fled the city altogether. But the majority of the residents, proud to have withstood eight years of fighting with Iran and confident of their ability to weather a conflict with the Americans, had simply gone about their business. Children who should have been evacuated from the city went to school as usual. Shoppers crowded the centuries-old bazaar on the left bank of the Tigris River. And at a horse track in Mansur, an upper-middle-class neighborhood to the west of the Rashid, men in long native gowns and flat caps clamored to place bets on the afternoon's races. The attitude of the bookmaker who collected their wagers was typical. "There will be no war," he predicted, waving a wad of twenty-five-dinar notes. "Nobody wants it."

Thus the antiaircraft fire must have come as a shock to him and most other residents of Baghdad. Not only were they at war, but as they were about to find out, they were facing an opponent armed with weapons that could strike with little warning and with uncanny precision, night or day. The first to reach Iraq were cruise missiles launched from guided-missile cruisers in the Persian Gulf and the Red Sea, more than 400 miles away. Using autonomous navigation systems, the missiles, called Tomahawks, tracked their progress over the wadis, highways, buildings, and other landmarks that passed beneath them, hewing closely to detailed flight paths stored in their computers. Then, carrying 1,000-pound high-explosive warheads for buildings like those struck in downtown Baghdad, they hit fifty-one targets throughout the country.

The cruise missiles flew too low to be detected by Iraqi air-defense radar. Chances are, the gunners who were deployed across Baghdad learned of the Tomahawks only when the first ones hit well-defended military installations and communications centers on the outskirts of the city. Aware of a threat but unable to see it, the Iraqis sent up the fireworks display Rankin watched from his ninth-floor hotel window. "You can imagine what was going through their minds," he said, "if they're sitting on a building trying

Early in the air war, muzzle flashes from three Iraqi antiaircraft batteries paint blacked-out Baghdad in garish light as tracer rounds cross the sky overhead. Because the stealth fighters that attacked the capital were virtually invisible to Iraq's air-defense radar, the gunners worked without early warning of the approaching aircraft and frequently opened fire only after the fighters' bombs had already hit home.

Iraqi gunners fire one of two Soviet-made ZU-23 antiaircraft weapons from a rooftop in Baghdad, startling a flight of pigeons. That the guns are active during daylight suggests that the crew is firing at a Tomahawk missile or perhaps a high-altitude reconnaissance plane rather than an attack aircraft, which flew against downtown Baghdad exclusively at night.

to optically sight an antiaircraft gun, and they're seeing ghosts and just blasting away at anything."

The lull that followed the initial assault was brief. After just five minutes, air-raid sirens sounded and the capital, including the Rashid, went dark. The second wave of the attack was spearheaded by batlike jet aircraft known as stealth fighters. Painted pitch-black and designed to penetrate enemy air space with little risk of being picked up on radar, the planes had approached Baghdad undetected. Then each one dropped a pair of 2,000-pound bombs and guided them to their targets by laser beam. When the bombs exploded, windows in the hotel rattled. At times, the entire building—a massive concrete structure that had been built during the war with Iran to withstand missile attacks—shook to its foundations, sometimes knocking Rankin to his knees. The concussions were deafening.

Listening to the din of the antiaircraft batteries, Rankin detected an unusual whooshing noise. Because it sounded so close to the hotel, he guessed that it was made by a cruise missile. He would not be certain until a daylight raid hours later, when he saw a dark gray Tomahawk flying just above the streetlights lining a highway near the hotel. The missile reached an intersection, banked, and continued up a different road, all the while emitting a tone identical to the one he had heard in the dark.

As the intensity of the night assault mounted, a fireball—possibly an errant Iraqi antiaircraft round—burst directly outside Rankin's window. The explosion and the cruise missile prompted him and other journalists to move to the hotel bomb shelter. There they found several hundred Iraqis, including many women and fearful children. Some in the crowd boasted that the Tigris was overflowing with the wreckage of American warplanes downed by Iraqi antiaircraft fire. Others played videotapes of pro-Saddam rallies and, clapping their hands, led the children in defiant chants of "Down, down Bush" and "Kuwait belongs to Iraq." But as tremors from the bombing coursed through the walls, word spread that the Presidential Palace and other government buildings had been heavily damaged in the bombing.

The news robbed even the most fanatical of their zeal. Nigel Baker, a British television producer who found sanctuary in the shelter at the same time as Rankin, marveled at the bombing's effect on Iraqi morale. "After hours of explosions outside," he said,

"they ended the night frightened into silence, their children clinging to them and crying."

When the bombing ended, around five o'clock, Rankin and other journalists sneaked past the Iraqis standing guard at the entrance to the shelter and went upstairs. The hotel, undamaged, was eerily silent. The electricity was off, and the bombing had severed all phone lines. As Rankin fumbled toward his room in the near dark, he scavenged rolls from room-service trays left in the corridor. At one point, he came across two Iraqi men pocketing packets of sugar, a commodity rationed during the trade embargo.

In his room, he discovered that the flow of water was dwindling. Quickly opening the taps before they ran dry, he filled as many glasses and empty beverage cans as he could gather. Later, guests wanting to bathe or flush toilets had to fetch water from the hotel swimming pool or a nearby fountain.

Correspondents looking down from the upper floors of the Rashid after daybreak reported an acrid haze in the air, broken glass in nearby buildings, and a column of thick smoke rising in the distance, but nothing that could be called devastation. "I expected to see outside my window a city in pieces," Baker recalled, "but there was no destruction in sight. Target hitting was precise."

Permitted to leave the hotel, Rankin saw only a few soldiers and civilians on the streets. Apparently, most of the residents of Baghdad remained fearful of venturing outdoors. Markets, shops, and restaurants were closed, as were all filling stations except those with hand-operated pumps. Traffic was sparse.

Despite the violence of the night just passed, Rankin saw little damage on his reconnaissance until he came to the Jumhuriya Bridge, a major thoroughfare across the Tigris that led to the old part of the capital. On the far riverbank to the north of the bridge stood a telephone switching station. More than a dozen microwave dishes mounted on top of the hulking concrete structure had caught his eye before the attack. He had assumed that the building would be a sure target in an air raid, and he was right.

From a distance, the communications tower appeared to be undisturbed. The building remained standing, antennas erect on its roof. Then Rankin noticed three clean, circular holes in one wall of the structure, seven or eight stories above the street. Each was about twelve feet in diameter. The installation appeared to have been hit by cruise missiles. Yet the many buildings standing nearby, including several high-rises, were unscathed. Witnesses reported similar scenes elsewhere in Baghdad, where government and military buildings located in residential neighborhoods were reduced to rubble while adjacent ten-story-tall apartment buildings were left largely undamaged.

It was learned later that the capital city was not the only target: A nuclear facility and air-defense installations across Iraq were also destroyed. Fighter aircraft were smashed in their hangars, and runways were cratered. Reinforced command-and-control bunkers were pierced and demolished. And missile sites throughout the country were shattered.

The Iraqi military had been sorely wounded in the opening hours of a campaign that coalition fliers would wage relentlessly for forty-two more days. Named Desert Wind, the aerial side of Operation Desert Storm was a massive, carefully scripted undertaking involving far more than the flurry of cruise missiles and stealth fighters that struck Baghdad and other targets the first night. Designed to ensure the defeat of the world's sixth-largest air force and fourth-largest army, the campaign would bring together thousands of aircraft with the aim of fulfilling the ultimate goal of any air force—to destroy an enemy's ability to fight effectively.

Defeating Iraq would require tens of thousands of tons of bombs, many falling on the roads, railroad lines, and bridges that linked the Iraqi troops in Kuwait with their supplies and reinforcements north of the Euphrates River. Still more were reserved for the Iraqi forces themselves, to wear them down in advance of the ground offensive that would prove necessary to expel Iraq from Kuwait. And the remainder would be delivered by warplanes providing close air support for coalition forces rolling northward from Saudi Arabia. Starring in the campaign would be so-called smart munitions such as the Tomahawk cruise missiles and guided bombs that opened the air war. But most of the ordnance dropped on Iraq and Kuwait consisted of simple, unguided bombs that differed little from those dropped during World War II. From H-hour, Baghdad, to February 28, the last day of the war, coalition warplanes rained down nearly thirteen times as many of these dumb bombs as smart ones.

Moreover, the great majority of aircraft that took part in Desert Wind were far from new. The stealth fighter, for example, had been operational for ten years before the bombing of Baghdad made it famous. Huge B-52s, some of them thirty years old, took part in the campaign from the first day. Like other aircraft of the Gulf War, these planes had been developed in response to a Soviet threat against Europe but were never employed as expected. Even smart weapons had a considerable history by the time of Desert Wind. Though never before used in a fight, the Tomahawk cruise missile was fielded in 1986, and the Air Force dropped its first laser-guided bombs on a North Vietnamese bridge twenty years before their descendants fell on Baghdad. Indeed, the panoply of aircraft, weapons, techniques, and tactics employed in Operation Desert Wind can trace its ancestry to the electronic age of warfare that began in the crucible of Vietnam during the mid-1960s and later extended to the Middle East and elsewhere. ★

The illustration below shows the relative ranges and coverages of the two basic types of air-defense radar. The wide fan of waves represents a long-range search, or acquisition, radar designed to detect incoming planes or missiles up to several hundred miles away. The antenna rotates continuously to illuminate the space indicated by the larger translucent bubble. A smaller bubble outlines the zone covered by a tracking, or fire-control, radar. Aimed at targets picked up by the search radar, it is limited in range to about fifty miles. More accurate than an acquisition radar, tracking radar directs gunfire or missiles toward a target.

Combat in the
Microwave Realm

Electronic warfare has become a critical contest that pits defenders trying to find and destroy approaching enemy aircraft against attackers intent on prevailing despite their efforts. Success in this arena can make the difference between victory and defeat and deserves much of the credit for the meagerness of the losses suffered by coalition air forces during Operation Desert Wind.

Dubbed the "wizard war" by Winston Churchill, electronic warfare is rooted in World War II and the introduction of radar, which measures distance to a target by noting the time needed for an echo of a radio signal to return to its source. Soon after the appearance of radar came efforts to neutralize it. One of the earliest antidotes was chaff, tiny metal filaments that, when scattered in the air, created a reflective screen that hid aircraft from opposing radar. Chaff is still used for that purpose—and as a last-second distraction intended to draw a radar-guided missile away from its intended target (pages 26-27). But more and more, combatants in this new kind of conflict fire salvos of electromagnetic pulses in an ever-escalating spiral of measure, countermeasure, and counter-countermeasure.

This type of warfare had its coming of age over Vietnam, where for the first time pilots had to fight in skies thick with radar beams and the weapons they guided. To meet the challenge, aircraft were fitted with computer-controlled electronic countermeasures (ECM) systems capable of instantly detecting radar signals, analyzing them, and determining the proper response. Such devices remain the basic tools of electronic warfare today, and only stealth aircraft—planes nearly invisible to radar—have no need for active measures to defeat it.

But for all others—and for defenders on the ground as well—there is no substitute for keeping one step ahead of the opposition. As shown on these and the following pages, each side has tricks up its sleeve, and the more inventive one side becomes, the more resourcefully the other must respond.

An Elementary Stratagem

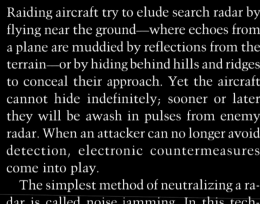

Raiding aircraft try to elude search radar by flying near the ground—where echoes from a plane are muddied by reflections from the terrain—or by hiding behind hills and ridges to conceal their approach. Yet the aircraft cannot hide indefinitely; sooner or later they will be awash in pulses from enemy radar. When an attacker can no longer avoid detection, electronic countermeasures come into play.

The simplest method of neutralizing a radar is called noise jamming. In this technique, an aircraft transmits a strong, continuous signal to overpower the faint echoes that the radar listens for. The result can be compared to trying to hear the tinkling of wind chimes amid an unremitting crash of cymbals.

This brute force approach to jamming exacts a toll in range, payload, or some of each, since supplying the electricity for shouting down multiple radars requires powerful generators that add considerable weight to the plane. Even with the largest dynamos that will fit aboard the aircraft, detection is only postponed. As an aircraft approaches a radar, echoes become stronger than the plane's jamming signal. At that point, which is known as burn-through range, the radar will hear the wind chimes in spite of the cymbals.

En route to a target, a fighter jams an enemy search radar by transmitting a powerful, continuous signal. On the radarscope, the jamming produces a cone of interference in place of the well-defined blip that would otherwise mark the aircraft's true position.

Falsifying the Distance to a Target

Caught in the gaze of a tracking radar, a pilot may have only seconds to live. Thus, an ECM system must respond quickly, before antiaircraft guns fire explosive shells to intercept the plane or SAMs rocket upward to chase it down. One antidote to the phenomenal accuracy of such antiaircraft weapons is to convince their radars that they are seeing a target where none exists.

A plane can sometimes confound a tracking radar by taking advantage of the opponent's narrow focus. When the radar is assigned a target, it registers range and bearing; it then estimates where the target will be when the next echo is received and pays attention only to echoes received from that area. Meanwhile, the plane's ECM system begins sending pulses that imitate the real echoes but are much stronger. Because the radar is designed to track the strongest signal, it follows the phony echoes rather than the real ones and directs gunfire or missiles to the phantom target.

After the radar has been lured off target—perhaps by as much as several miles—the aircraft turns off its jammer, and the radar screen goes blank. At this point the radar's human operator must intervene to reacquire the target.

Mimicking a real echo with a stronger signal transmitted a few microseconds later, a fighter paints a ghostly image that appears more distant than the actual aircraft. The ruse is aided by the radar; to avoid confusion, it ignores echoes coming from outside a box around a target, even a fraudulent one. On the scope, the false location appears as a blip; a silhouette marks the target's true position.

sidelobes used to deceive the radar as to
target's true bearing are the two less power,

A Case of Mistaken Direction

A companion to range deception is a jamming technique called bearing deception. In this ruse, a radar divines the distance to the target but is misled as to its direction.

The opportunity for this subterfuge lies in an unavoidable attribute of every radar antenna, called sidelobes—unwanted weak beams on either side of the powerful main beam. Radar engineers can minimize sidelobes but cannot eliminate them. Where they remain strong enough, suitable jamming equipment can exploit them to disguise a plane's whereabouts.

The deception begins when ECM gear detects a passing sidelobe. On subsequent passes, the jamming system generates a copy of a real echo, making it strong enough that the radar assumes it to be a main-beam echo and misjudges the plane's bearing.

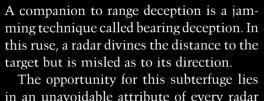

At left, a fighter sends spurious signals toward a distant radar as one of its sidelobes brushes past. Taking the false reflections as echoes of the main beam, the radar misjudges the direction to the target (*ghost aircraft*). On the radarscope (*below*), the silhouette indicates where the plane actually is, while the blip shows where the radar has mistakenly placed it.

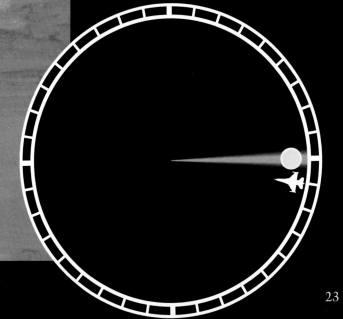

Radar's Rejoinder to Sham Signals

Range- and bearing-deception techniques can be nullified by ground radars that use a scheme known as frequency hopping. Instead of transmitting on a single wavelength, such radars skip around among scores of frequencies. Any attempt by an aircraft to create a ghost image with a single frequency fails because the radar can recognize impostor signals as differing in frequency from the real McCoy.

To counter this counter-countermeasure, ECM gear has to be just as nimble as the radar it is trying to defeat. Success is comparatively simple for radars that change frequencies at relatively long intervals according to a repeating schedule. Quicker switching and random hops among frequencies are more difficult to counter; the ECM pod cannot anticipate the next signal but must react instantly to whatever frequency arrives. To complicate matters further, the radar can transmit its pulses not singly but in patterns that can also vary. And so on.

Protecting an aircraft against such measures places a premium on ECM gear built around high-speed computers that can be reprogrammed between missions, if necessary, to counter the latest development on the electronic warfare front.

Pulses of different colors march from a frequency-hopping radar toward an approaching aircraft as the target attempts a deception using a single frequency. Occasionally, a false echo generated by the plane might match a radar frequency, but the radar will not be fooled. On the scope, the target appears as clearly as if it were attempting no countermeasures whatever.

A Last Chance at Escape

Even the most advanced jamming and deception techniques cannot always prevent an antiaircraft radar from directing accurate fire toward a plane. If the threat comes from antiaircraft artillery, the pilot must maneuver to avoid it. But against an approaching missile, other remedies exist.

The most common is to dispense chaff in the face of an oncoming weapon. Either the pilot or an automatic system aboard the aircraft releases clouds of these metal filaments, which reflect radar beams more brightly than the target.

A missile, however, is likely to be distracted only momentarily. Chaff has little momentum and slows rapidly upon release. The missile guidance system, recognizing that the chaff is traveling too slowly to be an aircraft, may resume tracking the real target. At that point, another cloud of chaff blooms, giving the missile a second false target—and so on. In a successful use of chaff, the missile passes well behind the aircraft or detonates as it nears one of the chaff clouds in the plane's wake.

A more dependable alternative to chaff is a decoy that is towed behind the aircraft. Planned for the mid-1990s, these devices operate both passively and actively. Such a decoy is shaped to offer a far brighter radar image to an oncoming missile than a fighter many times its size. To heighten its allure, the decoy also contains a transmitter that emits strong false echoes to the missile's guidance system (left).

Winged Chariots of War

An F-4C Phantom blasts a Vietcong-occupied hamlet in South Vietnam, spitting 2.75-inch rockets from six pods under the wings. The rockets—nineteen to a pod—were unguided and thus ill-suited for point targets. But a barrage from a flight of Phantoms could effectively saturate an area target. This payload was just one of many carried by the versatile Phantom, which could get right down on the deck to provide ground troops with much needed close air support.

Shortly after seven on the morning of June 5, 1967, Colonel Oded Merom of the Israeli Air Force lowered the canopy on his French-built Mirage IIIC fighter-bomber, acknowledged the raised thumb of his mechanic, and cranked up for war. Strapped in beneath the plastic bubble, anxieties soothed by the faint sound of the idling engine, Merom experienced a reassuring sense of being wrapped in a cocoon as he moved through his preflight routine. Releasing the brakes, he felt the delta-winged Mirage lurch forward slightly and begin to roll.

Moments later, the jet was streaking low over the blue sweep of the Mediterranean, turbulence in the wake of the plane whipping up foam on the choppy surface. Hugging the deck to elude Egyptian coastal radar, Merom led the three other Mirages in his flight westward over the ocean, then wheeled south, bound for the Nile Delta and the military airfield at Cairo-West. Parked alongside the runway there stood Merom's target: a row of Russian-built Tupolev Tu-16 bombers, each capable of delivering up to 20,000 pounds of explosives on Israeli population centers in the brief but intense conflict that was about to unfold. The pilot's responsibilities had been spelled out earlier that morning in an uncompromising battle order issued by Brigadier General Mordechai Hod, the forty-one-year-old commander of the Israeli Air Force (IAF). "Fly on," the general had urged his men, "attack the enemy, pursue him to ruination, draw his fangs, scatter him in the wilderness."

Hod's ardor signaled the gravity of the circumstances. For years, the IAF had been preparing for the worst—a war between Israel and hostile Arab powers on every side. In recent months, the stage had been set for just such a contest. Not only had Egypt concluded a mutual defense pact with Syria, but this strongest of Israel's enemies had also joined Iraq in dispatching troops to positions in Jordan near Israel's eastern border and evicted UN peacekeeping troops from the Sinai desert, thereby threatening Israel's western flank.

Military and civilian authorities in Tel Aviv had two options: to strike second or to strike first.

From General Hod's perspective, the advantages of throwing the opening punch were considerable. The IAF had fewer than 300 combat aircraft, while its Arab adversaries combined could deploy more than 700. A preemptive assault on the Egyptian Air Force (EAF) could eliminate the better part of that threat on the ground, Hod believed. The prime targets of the attack he had proposed to a receptive Israeli cabinet on the night of June 4 were Egypt's menacing strategic air force and its front-line fighters. The first consisted of an estimated thirty Tu-16 medium bombers and forty-five Ilyushin Il-28 light bombers; the fighters were MiG-21s, more than a hundred of them and a match for anything in Israel's arsenal.

To destroy the planes, the Israelis intended to exploit a critical laxity in Egyptian air defenses. MiGs patrolled the skies warily each dawn, but after they landed, none replaced them. Accordingly, Hod recommended launching the strike a few hours after sunrise on June 5, a time that might also catch top-ranking Egyptian officers on their way to work. Some radar installations were targeted, but the Israelis calculated that a pilot's best defense against Egyptian radar and SAMs was to come in perilously low—within forty feet of the ground—and pop up at the last minute to get a fix on the target. Above all, the operation would depend on surprise and coordination. Strict radio silence was to be imposed until the pilots reached their objectives, and the first wave of strikes was synchronized to descend on ten different airfields at precisely 8:45 a.m. Cairo time.

The cabinet had approved Hod's plan and now, as Colonel Merom approached the Nile Delta that morning, his formation close behind the first wave of attackers, he crossed a coastal lagoon. In boats below, fishermen looked up to wave. Within minutes, the Mirages had thundered across the Suez Canal unchallenged and were bearing down on Cairo-West. Merom could see smoke rising from the airfield, where the initial strikes had found their targets. He broke radio silence, ordering his pilots to full power for the attack. They had just enough fuel to complete four passes before dashing home—one to crater the runway with bombs and three to shred enemy aircraft with cannon fire. With his formation fanned out, Merom pulled back on the stick, sending his heavily loaded Mirage up to 9,000 feet before rolling into a dive. As he released his bombs on a runway littered with burning aircraft caught trying to take off, he saw a group of undamaged Tu-16s from the corner of his eye.

Wheeling low over the desert after the first run, the Mirages rushed toward the bombers. Merom later set down his impressions: "I come out of a shallow dive and the gunsight settles on a shining Tupolev. My finger squeezes the trigger on the column, the cannons roar and a burst of 30-mm shells rips through the bomber. It immediately catches fire and thick, black smoke begins to rise. A second and a third strafing run, and black pillars of smoke rise from all corners of the field." Merom's formation returned to its base unscathed, reporting the destruction of five Tu-16s.

At other airfields, the IAF was inflicting similar losses on the stunned Egyptians. Through the morning, wave after wave of raiders added to the carnage on Egyptian runways. After each sortie, the IAF pilots dashed back to base for ten minutes or so while expert mechanics deftly rearmed and refueled their planes. Then the fliers took off for another strike, reentering Egyptian air space less than an hour after they left it. This was an all-out effort; Israel held back only about a dozen aircraft to defend its homeland.

Within hours, Egypt's air force was in ruins, having lost more than 300 planes, including all thirty Tu-16s, twenty-seven Il-28s, and ninety-five MiG-21s. Syria, Jordan, and Iraq fared almost as badly, as Hod began to divert aircraft from the Egyptian front. Before the day was out, more than 100 aircraft belonging to Egypt's allies had been destroyed, and Israel, at a cost of just nineteen of its own planes, had gained air superiority.

Exploiting the advantage, the IAF provided close air support for the Army by attacking Arab forces that resisted the Israeli advance along the west bank of the Jordan River, in the Sinai, and on Syria's Golan Heights. Israeli pilots also flew interdiction missions, ranging far behind the lines to bomb and strafe supply columns and reinforcements. In Jordan, a brigade of advancing Iraqi troops was routed by low-flying IAF warplanes before it could join the battle. By the end of the Six-Day War on June 10, Israel had redrawn the map of the Middle East—and shown how a bold and unstinting application of tactical air power could alter the terms of battle.

Israel's lightning assault on the Egyptian Air Force, a textbook example of a so-called counter-air strike, was not without precedent in military history. As early as 1909, Giulio Douhet, an Italian staff officer and an astute prophet of air power, had declared that the primary objective of an air force in wartime would be to "deprive the enemy of all means of flying, by striking at him in the air, at his bases of operation, or at his production centers." The possessor of such dominance could range freely over the battlefield and disrupt enemy supply lines at will.

When war erupted in Europe in 1914, most aircraft were equipped only for reconnaissance and lacked the firepower or bomb-carrying capacity to play the decisive role Douhet envisioned. Nonetheless, within two weeks of the onset of hostilities, the Great War's first bombing attack, a counter-air strike, took place. On August 14, French aviators flying flimsy Voisin biplanes dropped small bombs by hand on the German Zeppelin sheds near Metz to put an end to the reconnaissance flights that the dirigibles had been making. This pioneering raid and similar forays in the months that followed inflicted little damage, but within two years both sides had deployed potent ground-attack aircraft sporting up to four machine guns and carrying more than a thousand pounds of bombs under their wings. Late in the war, air strikes dictated the outcome of several major ground battles—including an abortive Allied offensive at Cambrai in November 1917. In that action, the attacking troops advanced behind British tanks only to fall prey to strafing and bombing runs by low-flying German aircraft.

By the time war again engulfed Europe in 1939, Germany's Luftwaffe had developed the application of air power to the battlefield far beyond anything contemplated by its victims. Devastating counter-air strikes that September gave the Germans mastery of Polish skies within two days—a coup the Luftwaffe repeated the following spring by suppressing the French Air Force in forty-eight hours. In both cases, German air superiority, quickly established, subjected defending troops, tanks, and command posts to relentless assault from the air. Its chief agent was the dive-bombing Stuka, whose eerie shriek and uncanny precision epitomized the paralyzing impact of blitzkrieg.

Learning from the experience, the Allies ultimately amassed the warplanes and weaponry needed first to wrest control of the air from the enemy and then to dominate the battlefield from above. In the process, sturdy Allied fighter-bombers such as the American P-47 Thunderbolt and the British Hawker Typhoon, equipped with rockets that made up in punch for what they lacked in accuracy,

The ashes of three MiG-21s litter the tarmac of an Egyptian airfield following Israel's preemptive air strikes that opened the Six-Day War on June 5, 1967. By obliterating the bulk of the Egyptian Air Force on the ground, the raids nullified the Arabs' numerical advantage in warplanes and permitted Israeli pilots to challenge the Syrians and Jordanians at favorable odds.

reaped a bumper harvest of German tanks. Meanwhile, in the jungles of Asia and the South Pacific, the Japanese were prey to another lethal innovation—the napalm bomb, which created a fireball so demanding of oxygen that it most often killed by sucking the air from soldiers' lungs.

But these were as nothing compared to the weapons and aircraft that began to come of age two decades later in Vietnam. Often developed primarily with a view toward defeating a Warsaw Pact assault on Western Europe, then applied out of necessity to an entirely different style of conflict, these children were born of new technologies that were all but unheard of at the end of World War II: jet engines that could propel aircraft weighing more than some of the largest bombers of the 1940s faster than the speed of sound; navigation and night-vision systems for an unerring approach to the target; radars and computers that all but eliminated the guesswork from dropping bombs; and airborne weapons that could be guided to a target with never-dreamed-of accuracy. Yet none of these valuable novelties matured overnight, and even when they became commonplace, there remained a place for old-fashioned tactics and equipment.

A Crucial Airborne Middleman

Among those out front in the bitter contest that pitted Americans and South Vietnamese against the Vietcong and their North Vietnamese allies were the U.S. Air Force's forward air controllers, or FACs. "Nothing between them and the VC but air," a fighter pilot said of the FACs who sought out the enemy and directed close air support strikes. "No armor, no guns, no bombs. Just a light plane, a pair of good eyes, and guts." Operating over forested terrain that could make hostile forces hard to spot even during an engagement, the low-flying FAC was a throwback to the early days of military aviation, when reconnaissance was the main mission.

As if to underscore their traditional role, FACs operating over South Vietnam during the first few years of American involvement flew single-engine Cessna O-1 Bird Dogs, propeller-driven craft that differed little from observation planes flown during the Korean War and earlier. Cruising a few hundred feet above the trees at a top speed of 115 miles per hour, the poky O-1s were vulnerable even to rifle fire, prompting some pilots to fly in bulky, bullet-resistant flak jackets.

Had the enemy in South Vietnam possessed much at all in the way of antiaircraft artillery or any surface-to-air missiles, the airplane would have been utterly impractical. As it was, a post-flight inspection often revealed a fuselage pierced with bullet holes. In 1966, a year after the United States assumed primary responsibility for the campaign against the VC in the South, forty-eight of the 150 Bird Dogs operating in the region were shot down, and the toll might easily have been higher had it not been for the natural reluctance of the insurgents to reveal themselves by firing on reconnaissance planes.

Beginning in 1967, FACs began to take to the air in sturdier twin-engine craft, including the Cessna O-2 and the North American OV-10 Bronco, which had a cockpit sheathed in lightweight armor and carried a 7.62-mm machine gun for strafing "targets of opportunity." Over areas of Laos and North Vietnam where the threat from groundfire was much greater than it was elsewhere, forward air controllers flew jets. The speed of these planes, while making it harder to keep a target in view, also lowered to a tolerable level the risk that these so-called fast FACs might be shot down.

The Bird Dogs and their doughty successors proved indispensable in combating the VC. The pilots, sometimes taking off from crude airstrips hacked out of the jungle, patrolled the countryside, searching for the slightest signs of enemy activity—an unusually well

A forward air controller dives his tiny O-1 Bird Dog spotter plane toward the jungle and fires a white-phosphorus rocket from the right wing to mark a Vietcong position for fighter-bombers circling overhead. The pilot could also use colored smoke grenades strapped to the back of his seat to indicate troop locations—red for enemy, green for friendly. The M16 by his right knee was for self-defense should his thin-skinned, un-armed craft be shot down.

trafficked trail, newly constructed bunkers, or even troops in the open—that might presage an attack against a friendly installation or an ambush in the making. On other occasions, a FAC ranged ahead of friendly units on perilous search-and-destroy missions. His task was to ferret out the foe, if necessary goading the VC into venturing an AAA shot to reveal their position. If the FAC dodged the volley, he could summon often overwhelming firepower in the form of an artillery mission or an air strike. The call for air support was picked up by a command center on the ground or in an airborne C-130 Hercules transport. Controllers at this level then alerted the closest appropriate strike aircraft, whose pilot would usually contact the FAC for advice about sources of enemy fire before homing on smoke from a phosphorus rocket the FAC used to mark the target.

Frequently, the call went to an A-1 Skyraider, a Korean War-era prop-driven attack plane prized for such missions because, unlike a racy jet, it could linger several hours over the battlefield without exhausting its fuel. Together, Bird Dogs and Skyraiders made a formidable team, demonstrating that persistence and precision frequently counted for more than speed in the close-support role. In one instance, a FAC called in an A-1 to strafe a VC machine-gun nest within a hundred yards of friendly troops. "He rolled in and I held my breath," the O-1 pilot recalled. "I'm sure that the guys down there ducked their heads." With a brief burst from its four 20-mm cannons, the Skyraider silenced the enemy weapon.

In some circumstances, command centers might respond by sending in helicopter gunships or an AC-47, the attack version of the 1930s-vintage DC-3 transport. Given the radio call sign Spooky, this lumbering "gooney bird" carried three 7.62-mm Gatling guns that each unleashed a withering 6,000 rounds a minute. With an AC-47 overhead after sunset and parachute flares illuminating the landscape, American troops might be less inclined to agree with the rueful saying, "The night belongs to Charlie." But in the daylight, especially over well-defended positions, helicopters, AC-47s, and even the relatively speedy Skyraiders could fall to groundfire.

Where the enemy and their air defenses were thickest, however, the twin-engine F-4 Phantom, a supremely adaptable jet with a top speed of mach 2.0 that flew deep interdiction against the North, was often favored over the A-1. Hitting a small target from an F-4 streaking in at better than 500 miles per hour was a supreme test for the pilot and his weapons systems officer (WSO). "Without the aid

of radar computers for bombing," F-4 pilot Donald McDowell noted, "we had to mentally adjust for wind corrections. We could not just put our pipper on the target and pickle off the bombs."

F-4s usually attacked in pairs, allowing the wingman to learn from the lead fighter's bombing run like a golfer studying his partner's shot. Still, a single pass might not be enough to read the wind. Called in once by a Bird Dog to strike at VC troops established in a cave on a rocky hillside, wingman McDowell and his lead started out by making two unsuccessful runs each in an effort to drop 500-pound bombs accurately in a stiff breeze. "The FAC had marked the target's location with one of his smoke rockets," McDowell recalled. "Lead rolled in for his first dive pass. Two bombs departed the fighter as he initiated his pullout. Both bombs exploded 100 meters long of the target. My first two bombs hit fifty meters short. On our second pass he was short and I was long." With his last run, however, McDowell had the range: "I hit the pickle button releasing my two remaining bombs, and I eased the stick back into my lap. My nose was pointing upward into the blue sky when the FAC excitedly called out, 'You've hit the cave entrance, Two!' "

For all the grit and ingenuity of the airmen, flying close air support in the South could be disheartening. In tight spots, a slight miscalculation could mean death for friendly troops or civilians. Air-to-ground operations were tightly controlled to limit civilian casualties; Vietnamese province chiefs had to authorize strikes in

An A-1E Skyraider drops a white-phosphorus bomb on a VC-held village in September 1966. A seeming anachronism in an era of supersonic fighter-bombers, it was nonetheless the choice for many close-air-support missions in South Vietnam. Flying low and slow, it could linger over the target longer than the high-performance jets and deliver its payload more accurately.

populated areas. But when fighting erupted in or near hamlets, airmen might be called on to target guerrillas, who were hard to distinguish from noncombatants and sometimes used civilians as screens.

One such struggle occurred in 1965 at the town of Dong Xoai some sixty miles north of Saigon. There a Special Forces camp manned by fifteen Green Berets and a few hundred South Vietnamese irregulars was attacked by the VC. Outnumbered, the defenders called for air support. Soon UH-1 helicopter gunships, A-1 Skyraiders, and a host of other warplanes were raining fire on the VC positions. More than a thousand tons of explosives were dropped on the village and its outskirts. Aided by the barrage, a reaction force of South Vietnamese Rangers managed to lift the siege, but the air attacks had taken a frightful toll. Hundreds of friendly Vietnamese civilians were reported dead or missing.

In an effort to avoid such carnage, U.S. and South Vietnamese officials jointly designated certain areas in South Vietnam as free-fire zones. Civilians residing in these areas were moved to new homes, permitting FACs to call in air strikes on any activity in these areas without permission from higher authority. To deny the VC cover and sustenance in free-fire zones and elsewhere, the USAF dispatched spray planes to coat heavily forested regions and croplands with herbicides such as Agent Orange. More than a million and a half acres were defoliated in 1967 alone. Thereafter, concern over the ecological and health effects of the chemicals led the Pentagon to begin scaling back the program, but not before the disruption to peasant life caused by both the defoliation campaign and the free-fire zones was exploited by VC propagandists.

Such controversial efforts to alter the environment of Vietnam reflected the frustrations of American commanders, who were unable to gain as much as they expected from their unchallenged command of the air in the South. Operating in one of the least congenial settings imaginable for close air support, American pilots altered the outcome of countless small engagements but seldom had a chance to deal a crippling blow to enemy ground forces, who remained largely dispersed to avoid U.S. air power. The situation changed dramatically in late 1967, however, when North Vietnamese Army (NVA) troops entered South Vietnam in force. In mid-January of 1968, they launched an offensive that would provoke a display of American aerial firepower that the commander of U.S. forces in Vietnam, General William Westmoreland, termed "one of the heaviest and most concentrated in the history of warfare."

A Triumph of Air Power

More than 15,000 NVA soldiers had infiltrated the South and surrounded the vulnerable American base at Khe Sanh. Located in the western hill country just below the demilitarized zone (DMZ) marking the boundary between North and South, the complex of trenches and bunkers was served by an airstrip and garrisoned by 3,500 U.S. Marines and a few thousand South Vietnamese troops.

Khe Sanh had long been a thorn in the side of the Communists, situated as it was less than ten miles from Laos and the Ho Chi Minh Trail—the network of trails and roads that threaded southward from North Vietnam through eastern Laos and Cambodia. Westmoreland suspected that the North Vietnamese descending on Khe Sanh had bigger things in mind than simply neutralizing a threat to their supply lines, however. In his words, they appeared bent on transforming Khe Sanh into "another Dien Bien Phu"—a French garrison that had been besieged and conquered by the Communists in 1954, prompting France to withdraw from the region altogether. Determined to avoid a replay of that debacle, he drew heavily on the American fleet of 2,000 fixed-wing aircraft, ten times the number the French had deployed in Vietnam in 1954.

The first task was to keep the encircled troops at Khe Sanh fit and fighting by providing them with food, ammunition, and other supplies. Marine helicopters flew scores of resupply missions. Hulking Air Force C-130 transports made harrowing radar-guided descents through frequent clouds and fog to land on the 4,000-foot airstrip. Enemy antiaircraft gunners knew the approach flown by the transports by heart, and mortar and artillery crews had already zeroed in on the airstrip, so flying a resupply mission to Khe Sanh was hazardous duty in the extreme. To minimize exposure to hostile fire, the pilot touched down, turned onto a taxiway paralleling the runway, and quickly trundled toward a takeoff position. As the plane taxied, loadmasters in the cargo bay shoved pallets of supplies off a ramp at the rear of the plane. Reaching the end of the taxiway without ever having stopped, the rumbling transport turned onto the runway and took off through another gauntlet of groundfire. Despite such dangers, no C-130 was lost until February 10, when one crashed on the strip after being hit by machine-gun fire.

Subsequently, only smaller cargo planes—Air Force C-123s and C-7 Caribous—were permitted to land at Khe Sanh. But C-130s continued to make the run, resorting to an alternative delivery system that had been tried out at the base the year before while the runway was being rebuilt and extended. The pilot skimmed in as low as he dared, keeping the belly of the Hercules a few feet above the pavement. A parachute attached to each pallet and activated from the cockpit billowed out in the slipstream, dragging the load onto the runway. The C-130s still had to brave enemy fire, but by dropping out of the overcast at the last minute, maintaining speeds in excess of 100 miles per hour over the runway, and popping up into the clouds as soon as the last pallet was clear, the pilots gave the enemy gunners little chance to draw a bead on the transports. As one Hercules crewman described the maneuver, "we sort of sneaked in, made our drop, and made it out without getting hit."

While the airlift proceeded, Navy, Marine Corps, and Air Force attack planes pounded the North Vietnamese positions around Khe Sanh without letup. Five FACs patrolled the area in Cessna O-1s or helicopter gunships, pinpointing targets for warplanes that were stacked up over Khe Sanh like jetliners awaiting clearance to land at a busy airport. "These patterns sometimes extended up to 35,000 feet," noted an official Marine Corps report, "with scores of planes gradually augering their way downward as each preceding flight

A B-52D Stratofortress over South Vietnam drops a string of fifty-one 750-pound bombs to support U.S. ground operations in early 1966. As the war progressed, the mammoth, silvery bombers were repainted in a low-visibility camouflage pattern: green and brown on top to blend with the jungle foliage when viewed from above, with a black underside for bombing at night. Each plane required almost one ton of paint.

unloaded its ordnance and scooted for home." At night or in poor weather, Marine controllers in a radar van that had been flown into Khe Sanh and set into a protective revetment helped pilots fly toward a target at the correct speed to bomb from a safe height—around 14,000 feet—without seeing the ground. Accuracy was good enough to get the ordnance into an area the size of a football field.

The most dreaded weapon in the American tactical arsenal at Khe Sanh was an aircraft originally designed for a strategic role—the B-52 Stratofortress. Modified to carry up to 108 bombs weighing 500 pounds each—some of them hanging in huge bays built to hold nuclear weapons and the rest clustered under the wings—the B-52 had first been used for close air support in South Vietnam two years earlier. The previous November, three Stratofortresses, flying from a base in Thailand, unloaded their ordnance with devastating effect on enemy forces threatening the U.S. Marine base at Con Thien. Those bombs had fallen within a mile of friendly troops; at Khe Sanh, B-52s guided by ground radar routinely struck within a half mile of the perimeter. Observers on the ground rarely glimpsed the heavy bombers flying at 30,000 feet, but the carpet of explosions they unrolled and the unearthly glow of the blasts against the dark sky mesmerized the Marines and terrorized their opponents.

Marine Lieutenant Nick Romanetz recalled one such assault against an enemy-held ridge just over half a mile away: "It was still

overcast at the appointed time, and we all looked up into the sky. Nothing. But three or four minutes later we heard this eerie sound—a bubba-bubba-bubba sound like when you put a balloon on your bicycle wheel and the spokes hit it. Suddenly, the whole ridgeline exploded from one end to the other. It was a sight to behold, a mountain blowing up right in front of us." The B-52 raids, code-named Arc Light, killed many of those in the target area and left survivors dazed and demoralized. Reconnoitering after one such assault, Marines captured a single, dumbfounded North Vietnamese sergeant, all that remained of a battalion that had been swallowed up when the earth opened. The raid had come as such a shock that the sergeant could not even recall hearing the bombs explode.

To cope with smaller targets near the base, the defenders orchestrated miniarc and microarc lights—coordinated barrages by Army and Marine artillery, Air Force F-4 Phantoms, and Navy A-4 and A-6 Intruder attack planes launched from aircraft carriers in the Gulf of Tonkin. Indeed, any aircraft that could carry a bomb made an appearance at Khe Sanh. And through the night, Spookies circled above the enemy trenches like birds of prey, pouncing on anything that moved. "Every fifth round fired was a tracer," reported journalist Michael Herr, "and when Spooky was working, everything stopped while that solid stream of violent red poured down out of the black sky." The troops savored the show, Herr added: "You'd hear the Marines talking, watching it, yelling, 'Get some!' until they grew quiet and someone would say, 'Spooky understands.' "

The ability of the North Vietnamese to withstand such punishment for weeks on end awed the Americans. Lance Corporal Ray Nicol recalled: "We could see that trenches were being dug up to within fifty meters of the wire in some places. Napalm was dropped unignited and left to run into the trenches. Then the fighters came in and set the napalm off with rockets. After the grass burned off, we could see rats feeding on the enemy dead."

As the siege wore on, the once-verdant terrain around the base was stripped bare by the bombing. Craters abounded. When the wind was right, a stench of putrefying flesh wafted across Khe Sanh to mix with the aroma of gunsmoke from Marine artillery shelling the enemy in the hills. Finally, in early April, the battered North Vietnamese loosened their grip, and the Marines broke the siege. In seventy-seven days, more than 24,000 sorties had been flown and 100,000 tons of bombs expended, to secure one small but symbolic corner of South Vietnam.

Thousands of miles away in Washington, the results of the close-support missions in Vietnam offered insights to Pentagon planners who were looking beyond the conflict in Southeast Asia to a potential ground war with the Soviets in Europe and seeking aircraft to meet that most demanding of tests. The value of the B-52 as a tactical bomber had been convincingly demonstrated, and the Stratofortress would remain a prized asset for decades to come in the event of a conflict pitting U.S. forces against an entrenched foe.

Most analysts believed, however, that a future clash with the Soviets would be a fast-paced affair, and they sought attack planes that could take out mobile targets, notably tanks. Recent experience in Vietnam suggested strongly that, for close air support, maneuverability and endurance were more important than raw speed. Sending in high-performance jets such as F-4s to deal with small targets struck many observers as inefficient when the same job could be performed as well or better by slower aircraft that could operate from short airstrips close to the battlefield and linger there as a fight evolved. Indeed, some of the star performers on the close-support team in Vietnam were the slow movers—helicopter gunships, the AC-47, and the veteran A-1 Skyraider.

Convinced that choppers would be key to any future offensive operations, the Army embarked on a long-term effort to develop an attack helicopter that would lead to the introduction in the 1980s of the AH-64 Apache, a heavily armed tank buster with a range of 300 miles and a top speed of 180 miles per hour. In the meantime, the Air Force was designing a dedicated air-to-ground weapons platform of its own. As early as 1967, the Air Force had begun soliciting proposals for an experimental attack aircraft. The aim was to develop a somewhat speedier version of the efficient A-1 that would carry a bigger payload and be even more maneuverable than the Skyraider at low altitudes—as well as less vulnerable to groundfire. Its main implement against armor would be a 30-mm Gatling-type cannon capable of firing up to seventy rounds a second—one of the largest and deadliest guns ever carried by an aircraft.

The warplane that emerged from this competition in the early 1970s was the A-10 Thunderbolt II. Like its namesake of World War II fame, the plane was not pretty, and it soon had bestowed upon it the nickname Warthog. But pilots expert in flying close-support missions considered the new Thunderbolt more than satisfactory for its role. The A-10's two massive turbofan engines, hunched atop the fuselage behind the wings and away from the ground, provided the power needed to haul the fast-firing cannon, an additional sixteen thousand pounds of bombs or missiles, and a thick layer of titanium armor below the cockpit that could stand up to antiaircraft shells as large as twenty-three millimeters in diameter.

The Warthog saw no action in Vietnam, but other weapons that had been boiling longer in the pot emerged early enough to spark a transformation in the art of destroying targets on the ground from platforms in the sky. The arena was North Vietnam, the event an ongoing campaign of aerial interdiction known as Rolling Thunder.

Pounding the Enemy Heartland

"We split the North into six numbered sections that we called route packages," recalled Lieutenant Colonel Jack Broughton, vice-commander of the 355th Tactical Fighter Wing (TFW), based at Takhli, Thailand. The 355th was equipped with F-105 Thunderchiefs—heavy, hard-hitting planes known to pilots as Thuds for short. The Thud had been designed to deliver nuclear weapons against rear-echelon Warsaw Pact forces in the event of an assault on NATO. With bomb racks added under the wings and fuselage, it could carry a dozen 750-pound bombs.

"Package One was the southernmost," explained Broughton, a Korean War veteran who led Rolling Thunder air strikes beginning in 1966. "While defenses were lighter there, those who didn't properly respect them often paid with their lives for their carelessness. The significant targets and the tougher defenses were all to the north, and by the time you got to Pack Six, with Hanoi and Haiphong in the center, you were in the big leagues." Hanoi was the nexus for rail lines from the Chinese border and from Haiphong, North Vietnam's principal port. The capital was thus a funnel for weapons and other supplies destined for the insurgents in the South. "If you were an interdiction fighter pilot," Broughton noted, "Pack Six was what it was all about."

"Going Downtown," as Broughton and his fellow pilots referred to raids on Hanoi, was an excursion that made a stroll through the heart of the meanest of cities look like a cakewalk. Highly maneuverable MiG interceptors often lay in ambush. Hostile groundfire ran the gamut from small arms to 100-mm radar-aimed artillery. Every peasant, it seemed, had a weapon. "If we went low enough," Broughton remembered, "we could see them lying on their backs around the villages, firing straight up into the air." A single lucky rifle shot could rupture a plane's fuel or hydraulic line and condemn the pilot to death or years of harsh confinement in a North Vietnamese prison camp.

A greater threat was posed by antiaircraft artillery fire, which the pilots distinguished by the color of the smoke as the shells burst—"white for 37-mm, blue for 57-mm, and black with orange centers for the big ones." On some days, Broughton added, "the black stuff seemed to be everywhere, and if they were getting close you could hear and feel the detonations and see the orange core of explosion in the center of the black boxes. One hit or a close miss from one of those babies was enough."

To make matters worse, Hanoi was ringed with scores of launchers for SA-2 surface-to-air missiles. The radar-guided missiles, thirty-five feet long and about twenty-six inches in diameter, somewhat resembled telephone poles—except that they reached speeds in excess of mach 3 and could be encountered at any altitude up to 60,000 feet. SAMs sneaking up from behind were often dead-

Streaks of antiaircraft fire weave a deadly web above North Vietnam, vainly seeking the RF-4C reconnaissance plane that took this photo. Light antiaircraft artillery, the source of the cross fire seen here, spewed a continuous stream of fire, with every fourth round usually a tracer.

ly, but American pilots became adept at dodging the missiles when they were able to see them coming. The standard tactic was to lure the SAM into a dive, then climb sharply, a gut-wrenching maneuver that the missile usually could not match. Often it did not have to. North Vietnamese missile crews adopted the tactic of firing two missiles separated by a short pause. Successfully evading the first one could place a pilot in jeopardy from the second. Broughton, whose plane was nicked once by debris from an exploding SAM, recalled the experience: "The first sensation was the most god-awful noise I have ever heard. It ripped me way down in the bottom of my stomach someplace, like an old steam engine bursting out of a tunnel." It was all Broughton could do to complete his bomb run after the encounter. "Anyone who has been close enough to see and hear Sam's tail fire and feel the tickle of its fragments will tell you it's soul searing, or else he is a damn liar."

The Americans responded to the SAM threat in North Vietnam with a succession of increasingly sophisticated electronic countermeasures (ECMs). Most U.S. fighter-bombers carried external ECM pods that confused enemy radar; signals reflected by a formation of warplanes equipped with such devices would overlap on radar screens, making it difficult for the North Vietnamese to lock onto a specific aircraft.

Powering the pods was something of a problem. One early model relied on a propeller that rotated in the slipstream to turn the pod's generator, but the electrical output was slight, limiting the system's effectiveness; a later pod tapped the aircraft's power supply and did a better job of jamming radar signals. In addition, most American attack planes were equipped with gear that alerted pilots when they were being tracked on radar by emitting a shrill sound through the headphones and displaying the approximate bearing of the radar source on a screen.

To pinpoint and destroy radar installations, however, American commanders relied on special aircraft known as Wild Weasels because of their ability to ferret out the sites. Wild Weasels carried the costliest and most sensitive detection equipment. Electronic gear displayed the approximate bearing and intensity of enemy radar signals on a scope, distinguished between AAA frequencies and SAM frequencies, and warned of missile firings by listening for the telltale decrease in the interval between radar pulses that accompanied a launch. Keeping track of these systems was the job of the electronic warfare officer (EWO), who sat behind the pilot in the aircraft's backseat.

Pilot and EWO soon grew wise to the tricks of the North Vietnamese ground crews, who learned to avoid detection by turning on their radar just seconds before firing their missiles. In such cases, the Wild Weasel sometimes had to offer itself as bait and draw the enemy out. To compound the danger, the first aircraft deployed in this capacity in Vietnam, the F-100 Super Sabre, carried no weapons designed especially to destroy SAM sites; the crewmen had to attack the compact installations at close range with unguided iron bombs. In 1966, the Air Force came up with a new SAM buster—the Shrike missile, which could pick up an enemy radar signal and home on its source. The F-100, it was found, could neither keep up with the F-105s it was to protect nor accommodate the Shrike, so the Air Force looked to the larger, more adaptable Thud and devised a twin-seater version of the plane that was ideally suited to the task. Wild Weasels could now hold their own,

A battery of 85-mm antiaircraft artillery on the outskirts of Hanoi fires at approaching U.S. planes in October 1967. These guns could propel high-explosive, shrapnel-laden shells to an altitude of 30,000 feet. Batteries near the North Vietnamese capital were immune from attack under the restrictive American rules of engagement intended to spare the civilian population.

whether paving the way for fighter-bombers on regular missions or leading special sorties in which the Wild Weasel acted as the SAM-hunter while three conventional F-105s tagged along as killers.

On one such foray against Pack Six defenses that July, the pilot of the Wild Weasel had fired both his Shrikes at a SAM site when his EWO picked up the signal that another installation nearby was firing missiles. "Launch! We have a launch!" the EWO shouted into his microphone. The four pilots alertly broke formation and scattered in every direction. Dropping down low, the hunter caught sight of a pair of SAMs gaining on two of his killer escorts from behind and issued a timely warning. Then he spotted a third missile streaking toward his plane and had to take evasive action himself. Descending to treetop level, he waited for the SAM to follow, then pulled up sharply at the last second, dodging the warhead. The killers, meanwhile, had regrouped after their close call and spotted a sign of their prey—a dust cloud shrouding the SAM site that had fired on them. The target was theirs.

To the frustration of the pilots involved in Rolling Thunder, the technology for guiding bombs to objectives other than radar installations lagged behind that for targeting SAM sites. Most Thuds were equipped with an advanced radar both for navigation and for bombing. In the automatic-bombing mode, the pilot would put his pipper on the target and press the pickle button; the system would then release the bomb at the appropriate distance and altitude given such variables as the wind resistance of the ordnance and the speed of the aircraft. Yet the system was not foolproof. Strong, shifting winds could play havoc with the automatic mode, forcing pilots to revert to manual and make their own educated guesses as to when to release. To improve accuracy under such conditions, the Air Force and Navy developed so-called smart bombs or missiles with built-in electronic guidance and steering mechanisms.

These early smart weapons underwent a difficult debut in Vietnam. In April 1965, the Air Force launched a massive strike against the Thanh Hoa bridge, a hulking steel and concrete structure south of Hanoi that carried a major highway and rail line across the Song Ma River. The strike force included forty-six Thuds, sixteen of them armed with a pair of innovative guided missiles called Bullpups, whose flight path was governed by a small control stick in front of the mother ship's throttle. A pilot could unleash the Bullpup at a comfortable distance—up to five miles from the target—but then he had to eyeball the missile in, steering it toward the objective for more than thirty seconds, unable to maneuver to avoid intense AAA fire. Furthermore, only one missile could be directed at a time, so each Thud had to make two passes. Pilots hated the Bullpup, but time and again they threaded the needle and scored a number of direct hits—only to see the 250-pound missiles burst harmlessly against the thick piers. Plainly, larger warheads and a safer delivery system would be required to undermine major structures without significant losses.

Two years later, three Navy pilots flying A-4 Skyhawks from the aircraft carrier *Bonhomme Richard* in the Gulf of Tonkin struck the same bridge with a bigger and smarter weapon dubbed the Walleye, a glide bomb that was equipped with a television camera in the nose and steering fins. To drop the bomb, the pilot maneuvered his plane so that the target was centered on a cockpit display that showed the view from the Walleye camera, then pressed a button that locked the image in the bomb's guidance system. Upon releas-

A 750-pound general-purpose iron bomb, dropped by a U.S. Navy A-4C Skyhawk, falls toward North Vietnam. The target: a railroad bridge. Protruding from the nose of the bomb is a small wind-driven turbine that revs up after bomb release to arm the fuze as the weapon hurtles earthward. To ensure detonation, a second fuze is screwed into the rear of the bomb between the tail fins, which prevent tumbling and make the weapon fall nose first.

ing the Walleye, the pilot could take immediate evasive action while the bomb automatically steered itself toward a bull's-eye. This launch-and-leave capability, by enabling the A-4s to drop the Walleyes several miles from the Thanh Hoa bridge and beyond the range of the enemy antiaircraft-artillery batteries defending it, allowed the mission to be flown without the escorts that were usually needed to suppress air defenses. The bombs struck the bridge within five feet of each other, and the three Skyhawks returned safely to the carrier. But once again, the results were disappointing. For all their precision, the 1,000-pound Walleyes lacked the punch to demolish the structure.

It would take some time to develop weapons that had both the brawn to do the job and the ability to travel long distances to a target. In the interim, conventional blockbusters became the weapon of choice against North Vietnamese bridges.

Of even greater value than the Thanh Hoa bridge was the Paul Doumer Bridge, a vital artery that carried rail and road traffic from Haiphong and mainland China across the Red River into Hanoi. Named in honor of a former colonial governor of French Indochina, the nineteen-span steel bridge had, until early August of 1967, been off-limits to bombing because it lay within a restricted zone near the populous core of Hanoi. On August 11, thirty-six Thuds, each hefting a 3,000-pound unguided bomb, took off from bases in Thailand accompanied by four Wild Weasels and a like number of F-4 Phantoms.

Diving into the teeth of the capital's defenses at midday, the Thuds released their ordnance from an altitude of 8,000 feet or so.

An F-105D Thunderchief fires an AGM-12 Bullpup radio-guided missile at the Thanh Hoa bridge, one of the highest priority targets in North Vietnam. After launching the Bullpup, the pilot used its exhaust plume as a guide while steering the missile with a small joystick. When the Bullpup's rocket motor burned out after about twenty seconds, a flare on the tail ignited to serve as a visual reference.

During the raid, Wild Weasels took out two SAM sites and an 85-mm AAA battery in the area, but not before one aircraft, an F-4, was badly damaged when an 85-mm shell exploded near the cockpit, wounding the pilot. However, Captain Mike Messett, the WSO in the backseat, was uninjured. Operating duplicate controls, he nursed the crippled Phantom back to base.

The bombs tore up the bridge so badly that the North Vietnamese took six weeks to repair it. After that, bad weather permitted only intermittent follow-up raids for the remainder of the year. In all, Thuds flew nearly 150 additional sorties in a largely successful effort to keep the Paul Doumer Bridge out of commission. Yet the bridge was not destroyed, and aerial reconnaissance in January indicated that a few months of unhindered work by the enemy might yet put the structure back in business. As events turned out, the repair crews got the break they needed. Persistent cloud cover and winds precluded any further strikes that winter. And by spring, the Hanoi area was no longer subject to air raids, in part because of an offensive the Communists launched in the South on January 30 during a cease-fire called for Tet, the Vietnamese celebration of the lunar new year. In late March, President Lyndon Johnson, stung by domestic reaction to the Tet offensive and hoping to set the stage for a negotiated settlement, halted bombing north of the twentieth parallel, some 200 miles above the demilitarized zone and 75 miles below Hanoi. Seven months later, the president extended the moratorium to cover all of North Vietnam.

The 1968 bombing halt shifted the focus of the air interdiction campaign to the Ho Chi Minh Trail and Communist sanctuaries in Laos and Cambodia. Camouflaged seismic and audio sensors were air-dropped along the route to detect enemy troops and trucks, then fighter-bombers and B-52s were dispatched to attack them. However punishing, these raids failed to pinch off the flow of supplies and reinforcements to the South. When one route was cut, the Communists simply moved deeper into Laos or Cambodia. Enemy pressure persisted on South Vietnamese troops, to whom the United States was gradually turning over the burden of defending their territory.

Some veterans of Rolling Thunder remained convinced that interdiction against the North was the only way to stop the Communist advance and lamented the lost opportunity. Pilots looked

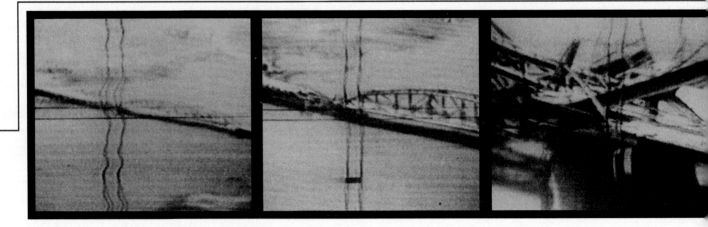

back ruefully on missions they felt had been all too predictable. Lacking sufficient forces to mount strikes around the clock, operational planners had fallen into the habit of administering fixed doses of air power at regular intervals, so that the airmen sometimes returned repeatedly to a target from the same direction and at the same hour, sacrificing the advantage of surprise. To make matters worse, the Air Force and the Navy seldom coordinated the efforts of their strike forces, so that some missions were redundant while others failed to achieve their intended effect for lack of a quick follow-up.

But above all, the pilots bridled at the restraints placed on them by officials in Washington who feared the political and diplomatic consequences if they gave commanders in the field free rein to select their targets. President Johnson, intent on avoiding the onus of devastating civilian areas or harming Russian or Chinese vessels or personnel, approved all the targets himself and left the fighter-bomber pilots little latitude in planning their missions. "President Johnson was serious when he said that we couldn't even hit an outhouse without his permission," Colonel Broughton complained. "We knew we were better qualified to sort out outhouses at five hundred knots than Johnson was, especially when those outhouses were shooting at us."

Behind the misgivings of the president and his subordinates lay persistent doubts about the accuracy and effectiveness of tactical bombing. Washington had been disturbed not only by the protests that the strikes stirred up at home and abroad but by the cost of the interdiction campaign. By official estimate, it had taken twenty tons of bombs to destroy one ton of matériel bound for the South—a poor return on an investment that exhausted not only ammunition but aircraft and pilots. In three years, 1,203 airplanes were shot down, most of them over North Vietnam or Laos. Such liabilities of the deep-interdiction option would persist until pilots had weapons accurate enough to reduce the likelihood of collateral damage and eliminate the need for hundreds of high-risk sorties to destroy a single major target.

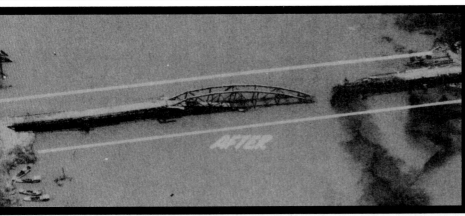

The three pictures at far left show North Vietnam's Ninh Binh bridge through the television camera mounted in the nose of a Walleye glide bomb, as seen by a fighter-bomber pilot on a cockpit monitor. The pilot aims the weapon by positioning on the target a small box formed by intersecting horizontal and vertical lines in the center of the image. After release, the weapon's on-board guidance system steers it to impact, freeing the plane to take evasive action. The fourth photograph shows the result of the successful strike.

In the spring of 1972, President Richard Nixon responded to a fresh North Vietnamese ground offensive in the South with Operation Linebacker, a renewal of the air-interdiction campaign against the northern heartland. High on the list of targets once again was the Paul Doumer Bridge, rebuilt and protected by an even stickier web of defenses than before. "We had this big map of North Vietnam, with all the high-threat areas marked in red," recalled one Phantom pilot engaged in Linebacker. "Well, almost the whole damn map was red. I don't know why the intelligence people bothered. They would show a little corridor we could squeeze through where there was a medium-threat area, but we might have to go two hundred miles out of our way to do that. It got to be a joke, because either you joke or you cry about a thing like that."

However, the pilots held an extra ace or two. During the long hiatus in the air war against the North, research and development had proceeded on heavy smart bombs intended to make raids on well-defended targets in populous areas not only less hazardous and more precise but more effective, too. One type was essentially an update of the 1,000-pound television-guided Walleye, but with a warhead twice as large. A second class was a new breed of smart explosives—laser-guided bombs (LGBs)—which homed on a point illuminated by a pencil-thin laser beam. Dumb bombs weighing up to 3,000 pounds could be converted to laser-guided ones simply by fitting the nose with steering vanes and a laser sensor that sought out the point lit by the beam.

To train the laser on the target, the Air Force equipped a number of F-4 Phantoms with an elaborate and somewhat awkward system known as Pave Knife. A pod beneath the wing contained the laser and a television camera. Both instruments were aimed from the backseat by the WSO, who pointed a gimbaled televiewer at the target. The goal was to keep cross hairs in the apparatus positioned on the objective until the bombs arrived, meaning that at least one aircraft in the formation had to circle and mark the objective while the others unloaded their ordnance and made a quick getaway. The designers were confident that the pinpoint accuracy of the LGB would more than compensate for its limited fire-and-forget capability—but they were not flying the airplanes.

To bring these assets to bear against the stoutly defended Paul Doumer Bridge, the Air Force relied heavily on the swift F-4, supported by F-105s in the Wild Weasel role. Early on May 10, sixteen Phantom bombers—four carrying a pair of 2,000-pound Homing Bomb Systems (HOBOS) television-guided bombs each and the rest hauling two 2,000-pound LGBs each—took off from bases in Thailand. Clearing the way for these aircraft and for a similar force that was scheduled to strike Hanoi's Yen Vien rail yard around the same time were Phantom fighters to patrol for MiGs, followed closely by Wild Weasels to soften up the surface-to-air missiles; other F-4s to sow the skies over Hanoi with chaff, metallic strips that shrouded aircraft from radar's prying eye; and four EB-66s—special electronic-warfare planes—to conduct high-intensity jamming of enemy SAM and AAA radar from a distance *(pages 18-19)*. Altogether, eighty-two aircraft were going downtown in one of the most complex raids of the war.

Alerted by early-warning radar, a swarm of MiGs bounced the lead Phantom fighters soon after they crossed the North Vietnamese border, and a fierce dogfight ensued. One Phantom went down, but the Americans destroyed three MiG-21s and chased off the rest, allowing the Wild Weasels and the radar-jamming aircraft to reach their objective on schedule, around a quarter to ten. The EB-66s began to circle fifty miles from Hanoi at 30,000 feet and emit their powerful signals. Meanwhile, the chaff spreaders flew straight in at 23,000 feet, presenting a tempting target for SAMs. One backseater, Lieutenant Lanny Toups, warned of a SAM launch by gear aboard the plane, alerted his pilot, who went into a steep dive. "Just about the time we started down, the missile detonated," Toups recalled, "and the blast turned us upside down." Even so, the pilot righted his plane and released his chaff in concert with the three other F-4s.

The metallic confetti screened not only the approaching strike aircraft, but the Wild Weasels as well. They were having a field day. "We didn't have any SAMs fired at us," observed flight leader Lieutenant Colonel James O'Neil. With the chaff dispensers serving as unintended decoys, O'Neil's Thuds unloaded at will on the SAM sites. But they could only make a dent in the city's defenses, considerably beefed up during the long suspension of bombing.

A few minutes before ten, the Paul Doumer Bridge strike force approached Hanoi, streaking in over the Red River from the south. "Visibility was good and you could see the SAMs for miles," remarked Colonel Carl Miller, leader of the flight carrying the HOBOS. "That is the main thing I remember about that mission, the vast number of SAMs going over us, under us, in front of us, behind us." Thanks to the chaff and the EB-66 jammers, few missiles were homing, and the incoming fighter-bombers were able to maintain formation. The AAA batteries were spitting an enormous volume of fire as well, but the standoff capabilities of the TV-guided bombs enabled the pilots to stay above and beyond the worst of the flak. Miller's flight pickled off their ordnance at 12,000 feet, with the bridge still five miles distant. But the picture-book delivery ended on a sour note as the TV-guided bombs went haywire. One of Miller's made a ninety-degree turn and exploded near the train station in downtown Hanoi. "I don't know where the other went," said the colonel. The complex visual background of Hanoi may have confused the bombs' guidance system, which could be distracted by shapes and contrasts that mimicked the target selected. Later TV-guided bombs would be more discriminating.

It was a different story with the laser bombers. Each flight of four attacked in two pairs separated by about fifteen seconds. The flight leader, up front with his wingman, had the unenviable task of releasing his own bombs and then circling with the bridge in view so that his WSO could mark the target with the laser beam until the bombs delivered by all four Phantoms in the flight hit home. The laser and TV camera in the Pave Knife pod were trained straight ahead as the lead plane zeroed in, so the WSO had a clear view of the bridge through his scope and could pinpoint the target with the beam. But once the pilot pickled off and began to circle, the WSO had to make a quick adjustment and retain the target in his scope or the bombs would go astray. Fortunately for the vulnerable target-designator, the big AAA batteries, which had the range to reach the Phantoms above 12,000 feet, were anticipating the same kind of attack launched against the bridge before the bombing halt. "The Vietnamese gunners obviously expected us to release from a lower altitude," explained Captain Lynn High. "They coned their fire on a point 7,500 to 9,000 feet above the target. It looked like an Indian tepee sitting over downtown Hanoi." Staying well above the cone, the markers kept their lasers focused steadily on the bridge as the bombs arrowed in and detonated.

Captain Mike Van Wagenen, with the last pair of LGB-laden Phantoms, could see thick columns of smoke and debris rising from the bridge as he approached close behind his flight leader. He thought at first that the bridge had been wrecked, but a closer look told him otherwise: "That sucker was still standing," he marveled afterward. Flying in the plane alongside Van Wagenen was Captain Mike Messett, the former backseater who had taken control of a wounded Phantom during the 1967 strike and guided it home. "I had a long unsettled grudge against that bridge," Messett confided. Now he was taking revenge. As Van Wagenen entered his dive, he focused exclusively on the target and filtered out all other sensations: "The radio seemed to go quiet, the radar warning gear went quiet, everything appeared to go quiet as I tracked the Doumer Bridge underneath my sighting pipper. We just stopped thinking about the other things going on around us. My backseater was calling off the altitudes: fifteen . . . fourteen . . . thirteen. . . . The pipper was tracking up the bridge, I had the parameters like I wanted them and released both bombs." Pulling up, he became acutely aware once again of the shrill sounds of battle—"it was like plugging in the stereo."

All four of the LGBs released by Van Wagenen and Messett exploded against the eastern end of the bridge, but the outpouring of smoke prevented the pilots from sizing up the damage as they broke away. Post-strike reconnaissance revealed that the bridge had been rendered unusable by the raid, with several spans severely damaged if not actually dropped into the river. Most of the LGBs had struck the target, and all of the fighter-bombers had weathered the storm, profiting by their remote-delivery technique. Intent on finishing off the bridge, the Air Force sent Captain Messett back to Hanoi the next day with a much smaller strike force assembled around a quartet of Phantom bombers, one of them armed with a pair of 3,000-pound LGBs and the rest with 2,000-pounders. Defenders appeared to be caught off guard by the quick follow-up, and groundfire in the vicinity of the bridge was surprisingly light. The run went like clockwork, and the LGBs hit dead-on. Reconnaissance photographs showed three spans down, and several others mangled. The Paul Doumer Bridge was out of business for the remainder of the war. Two days later, a smart-bomb raid knocked a gaping hole in the Thanh Hoa bridge.

In the weeks and months that followed, repeated American air strikes stymied the Communist offensive. Under the pressure, Hanoi endorsed a cease-fire in January 1973. The agreement enabled the United States to make a face-saving exit from the conflict, but it left North Vietnamese troops in place in the South—poised to renew hostilities at Hanoi's bidding. On April 30, 1975, Saigon fell to the Communists. America had lost.

A Bright Side to a Gloomy Story

Among the facts beclouded by the defeat was that the United States Air Force in the mid-1970s was in better condition than it had been since World War II. Not only had the war in Vietnam sharpened the skills of pilots and endowed them with deadly new weapons systems, but the USAF was well along the way toward modernizing its fleet of tactical aircraft. Most of the planes deployed to Vietnam had been designed in the 1950s, and few were suited to the USAF's main mission in any future war: to fly interdiction missions—to destroy enemy command-and-communications centers, to blast tanks and troops before they could reach the front, to do all that was possible, in short, to keep friendly ground forces from becoming mired in battle. Such a head-on clash with the Soviets in Europe might be catastrophic, since the United States and its NATO Allies lacked the forces to match the Russian army. In the event of war, the first task of NATO warplanes would be to disrupt that army before it could gain momentum, thus precluding a massive frontal assault that might leave the Allies with a terrible choice—to yield territory or to retaliate with nuclear weapons.

In such circumstances, the USAF would be spread thin and would not have the luxury of directing massive strike forces against high-priority targets as in Vietnam. Fortunately, advances in electronic countermeasures technology and other avionics—compact circuitry that helped pilots fly the aircraft, deliver weapons, and evade enemy fire—were making it possible for a single plane or a small strike force to accomplish a mission that would have required scores of attack planes a few years earlier. The first of these smart planes—the F-111—had entered operation in time to play a small role in the Vietnam conflict. But its significance went far beyond that war. By demonstrating that computers could routinely and reliably perform functions beyond the capacity of one—or even two—unassisted crewmen, the F-111 paved the way for a new generation of attack aircraft whose electronic systems responded swiftly and intelligently to the challenges of combat and allowed for deep strikes into well-defended territory without a host of escorts.

Although the F-111 was equipped with two radar-jamming pods like the ones carried by the Thuds and Phantoms, its main defense against detection was an ability to cruise for long distances below the effective radar coverage—generally around three or four hundred feet above the ground. Such low-level flying was a standard tactic for interdiction—one that Israeli pilots had worked to perfection on the first day of the Six-Day War. But hugging the deck in this way for extended periods, with the aircraft plowing through dense, often turbulent air, could be taxing on the nerves. At the very least, pilots joked, "you could get your eyeballs shaken out." And any number of conditions—including uneven terrain, poor weather, and dwindling daylight—could render low-level flight prohibitively dangerous. The genius of the F-111 was its capacity to follow the contours of the roughest landscape, even in dense fog or the depths of night, and drop its payload accurately on an invisible target.

In part, the F-111 owed its remarkable performance to a novel design feature—wings that swept back after takeoff to cut wind resistance and stabilize the aircraft in low-level flight. But its most important asset was a terrain-following radar navigation system, whose computer analyzed data from an antenna scanning the landscape miles ahead and commanded the aircraft to rise, descend, or turn, depending on the circumstances. If the radar detected a tall, narrow obstacle such as a broadcasting tower, for example, the computer would instruct the plane to go around it rather than over it. The two-man crew of the F-111, seated side by side, would determine the basic flight plan and adjust the speed, and the computer would do the rest—unless the pilot elected to switch to manual.

The experience of riding in an F-111 on the deck, in the dark, made an impression. "Think about flying around in daylight and good weather only 200 feet above the ground, going up and down over hills and into valleys," remarked Captain Jackie Crouch, who flew the F-111 in Vietnam. "Now do this at night, in mountains and in heavy cloud when you can't see anything outside the cockpit. This is really, really exciting, even without the enemy threat."

Initially, the F-111 relied on radar for night bombing as well. The WSO would pick up the target image on a scope in the cockpit and

An F-111 fighter-bomber, used in the surprise raid against Libya on April 15, 1986, rests in its hardened shelter at RAF Laken-heath airfield. Though the curved metal roof is covered with a thick layer of reinforced concrete and heavy blast doors at both ends of the shelter protect the plane against a near miss, such structures are largely obsolete in an era of precision bombing.

lock onto the aiming point with the cross hairs; an on-board ballistics computer would then release the bombs at the proper range. Although Vietnam war-horses such as the Thud had automatic radar bombing, the F-111 was more precise in this mode because it incorporated data from the plane's innovative inertial navigation system (INS). The INS used gyroscopes and other sensors to detect the slightest change in the plane's momentum, and it was further able to distinguish between changes caused by acceleration and those caused by shifts in the wind. This extraordinary sensitivity to the movement of the aircraft and to the force of the wind allowed the F-111 to deliver dumb bombs with an accuracy approaching that of smart weapons. Then, in the early 1980s, the Air Force modified some F-111s to accept an ingenious pod known as Pave Tack that made it easier for the WSO to aim the laser for bombs dropped by his own aircraft. The pod, which also contained a forward-looking infrared (FLIR) sensor, descended from the main weapon bay during an attack. Using the infrared scope to find the target, the WSO then centered the laser cross hairs on it, waiting to turn on the beam until the pilot had released the LGB. At this point, the plane could break away and the pod would swivel automatically to keep the laser and FLIR focused on the target, eliminating the need for the aircraft to hold steady until the bomb hit.

Pave Tack made the F-111 a deadly night stalker. Such was the Air Force's faith in the plane that when President Ronald Reagan decided in 1986 to authorize a strike against Libyan strongman Muammar al-Qadhafi in retaliation for his sponsorship of terrorism, a squadron of Pave Tack-equipped F-111s was dispatched from England to join in the raid. Because both France and Spain had denied U.S. warplanes access to their air space for the operation, the mission required a circuitous 2,800-mile trek around Gibraltar, with four in-flight refuelings. After a flight of more than seven hours, several F-111s streaked in low over Tripoli in the darkness at 500 knots and blasted Qadhafi's compound and a terrorist training facility outside the city with 2,000-pound LGBs. One F-111 went down in the operation, which included strikes on Libyan military targets; the rest returned safely to base. The fifteen-hour mission left some crewmen so stiff they had to be lifted from their seats.

When the F-111 raided Tripoli, it was just one of several smart planes in the U.S. arsenal. A heavy aircraft designed for furtive thrusts into enemy territory, the F-111 had limited air-to-air capability and was never intended to fill the versatile role played in Vietnam by the F-4 Phantom. Indeed, late-model F-4s remained on the American roster through the 1980s, primarily for reconnaissance and Wild Weasel duties. But as early as the 1960s, plans had been laid for two smart successors to the Vietnam-era Phantoms— aircraft that would combine raw power and exceptional maneuverability with advanced navigation and weapons delivery systems.

One of them was the F-16 Fighting Falcon, conceived from the start as a multirole fighter-bomber. The F-16, which became operational in 1979, incorporated a single engine, yet the Falcon's compact design and lightweight construction gave it a top speed of mach 2 and great agility, making it superior to the MiG-21 and competitive with more advanced Soviet fighters. A single-seater, the F-16 was loaded with avionics to shoulder some of the work load of the WSO in a two-seater. Computers linked to electronic, fly-by-wire controls—the first use of such a system to replace hydraulic controls in an American warplane—kept the racy little jet manageable. A new head-up display (HUD), valued for its wide field of view, translated all the essential data from radar, navigation, and attack systems into symbols. Exhibited on a transparent screen, the information enabled the lone pilot to monitor his weapons systems during dogfights or ground strikes without averting his gaze.

The automatic bombing system on the F-16 was similar to that on the original F-111 but even more accurate. It had an improved INS and a more powerful computer to process data faster and therefore calculate bomb impact points more precisely. This package, which raised dumb-bomb delivery to new heights of precision, was known as the two-mil system because it promised an error of no more than two feet for every thousand feet separating the target from the release point.

The other new strike aircraft was a variant of America's premier fighter, the F-15 Eagle, which had entered service in 1974. The designers of the Eagle, which had a top speed in excess of mach 2.5, were so intent on keeping it sleek and fast for air-to-air combat that it was said they had added "not a pound for air-to-ground." But the jet's twin turbofan engines provided so much thrust that the design was easily modified to carry the heavier loads required of attack aircraft without sacrificing much in the way of quickness or agility. To monitor the extra radar and delivery systems required for the air-to-ground role, the Strike version of the Eagle—the F-15E, introduced in the 1980s—added a backseat to accommodate a WSO.

Ultimately, in the late 1980s, both the Strike Eagle and the Fighting Falcon would become even keener predators with the help of a new system for low-level and night navigation, known as LANTIRN, which projects an infrared image of the target area onto the pilot's HUD (pages 64-65).

Nicking Iraq's Nuclear Balloon

Long before the arrival of LANTIRN and the F-15E, however, the adaptable F-16 became a mainstay of the USAF and much sought after by America's allies. Among the first nations to receive F-16s was Israel, and in June of 1981, Israeli pilots offered a stunning demonstration of the Fighting Falcon's deep-strike capability.

For some time, Israeli intelligence had been monitoring construction of a French-designed nuclear-research reactor near the Iraqi capital of Baghdad. The Israelis feared that the facility, designed ostensibly for peaceful purposes, would be used to produce plutonium for atomic weapons, providing Iraqi leader Saddam Hussein with the means to make good on his repeated threats against the Jewish state. Reports indicated that the main reactor would be activated in the summer of 1981. The government in Tel Aviv decided to destroy the facility before its core became radioactive.

In planning the delicate operation, the IAF decided to use F-16s carrying dumb bombs. There was little doubt that the planes had the accuracy to hit the fifty-foot-wide reactor dome, especially if they released their bombs from an unusually low height for such a mission—4,000 feet. To be sure, the risks of such close-range bombing were considerable, but the IAF trusted in the skill of its pilots and in the smarts of the Fighting Falcon.

Two flights of four F-16s would make the 650-mile run to Baghdad. Each aircraft would carry a pair of 2,000-pound iron bombs along with ECM and chaff pods, two Sidewinder air-to-air missiles, and 14,000 pounds of fuel, much of it carried in external tanks that would be jettisoned along the way. Once aloft, the jets would fly low to evade radar and slow to conserve fuel. With the extra weight, they would be vulnerable to MiGs, so six Israeli F-15 air-superiority fighters were assigned to escort them.

The strike force took off from Etzion airstrip in the Sinai on June 7 at 3:00 p.m.—a departure time that would bring the bombers in on the target from the southwest in late afternoon, with a blinding sun behind them. As Lieutenant Colonel Ze'ev Raz, leader of one of the two F-16 flights, started slowly down the runway, he won-

Iraq's Osirak nuclear reactor—target of a surprise surgical strike by Israeli F-16s on June 7, 1981—is shown here in October 1980. Only weeks before this picture was taken, the Iranian Air Force had attacked the installation, prompting the Iraqis to beef up their security and air defenses. The Iranian air raid damaged some labs and service facilities but missed the reactor itself, situated under the large white dome.

dered if the load would prove too much for the single-engine jet. After rumbling along for 4,000 feet, it was still shy of 150 knots. Raz, accustomed to lightning takeoffs, likened the experience to riding a giant tricycle. But at 5,200 feet, he gave the stick the slightest pull as prescribed and inched the nosewheel off the pavement. Obediently, the Falcon eased into the air.

Soon both flights of Falcons and their escorts were off the ground and crossing the Gulf of 'Aqaba into Saudi Arabia, pursuing a course that threaded a gap between Saudi and Jordanian radar coverage. Skimming the desert at an altitude of 100 feet, the jets entered Iraqi air space unchallenged a little after 5:00 p.m. and checked their instruments for the attack. Switching hands on the stick, Raz felt behind him with his right hand to set switches that programmed his chaff pod to release two bundles of the strips each second during the ten seconds or so it would take him to pop up and dive toward the target. Then he reviewed the status of his weapons systems on the HUD. A symbol reminded him that the pickle button on his

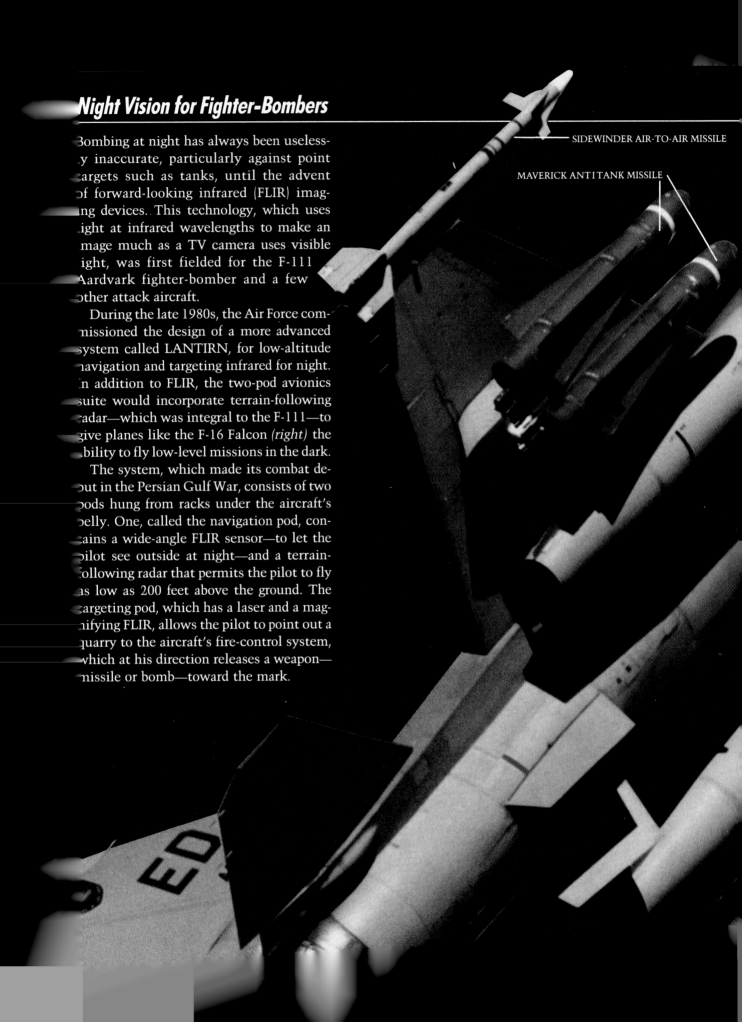

Night Vision for Fighter-Bombers

Bombing at night has always been uselessly inaccurate, particularly against point targets such as tanks, until the advent of forward-looking infrared (FLIR) imaging devices. This technology, which uses light at infrared wavelengths to make an image much as a TV camera uses visible light, was first fielded for the F-111 Aardvark fighter-bomber and a few other attack aircraft.

During the late 1980s, the Air Force commissioned the design of a more advanced system called LANTIRN, for low-altitude navigation and targeting infrared for night. In addition to FLIR, the two-pod avionics suite would incorporate terrain-following radar—which was integral to the F-111—to give planes like the F-16 Falcon *(right)* the ability to fly low-level missions in the dark.

The system, which made its combat debut in the Persian Gulf War, consists of two pods hung from racks under the aircraft's belly. One, called the navigation pod, contains a wide-angle FLIR sensor—to let the pilot see outside at night—and a terrain-following radar that permits the pilot to fly as low as 200 feet above the ground. The targeting pod, which has a laser and a magnifying FLIR, allows the pilot to point out a quarry to the aircraft's fire-control system, which at his direction releases a weapon—missile or bomb—toward the mark.

SIDEWINDER AIR-TO-AIR MISSILE

MAVERICK ANTITANK MISSILE

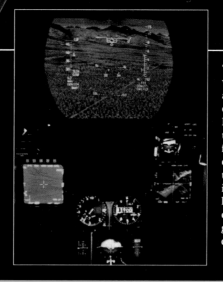

FUEL TANK

The navigation-pod FLIR provides an image of the terrain ahead that appears on the aircraft's head-up display (HUD). Near the top is a box drawn by the navigation pod's terrain-following radar. By keeping a circular symbol of the jet within the box, the pilot avoids crashing. Below the HUD and to the left is a targeting screen with cross hairs for designating targets. A third screen shows a radar image of the ground.

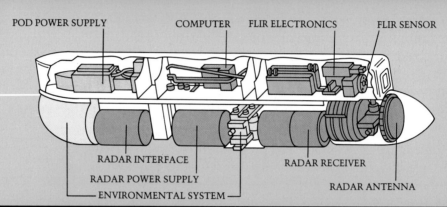

POD POWER SUPPLY   COMPUTER   FLIR ELECTRONICS   FLIR SENSOR

RADAR INTERFACE   RADAR RECEIVER

RADAR POWER SUPPLY   RADAR ANTENNA

ENVIRONMENTAL SYSTEM

The Navigation Pod. On the upper level are a power supply, a computer, and a FLIR sensor that provides an image of the world outside the cockpit. On the lower level are components of the terrain-following radar, including an interface unit linking the pod with the plane's autopilot. An environmental control system keeps heat-sensitive electronics from burning out.

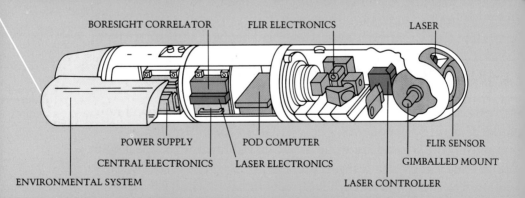

BORESIGHT CORRELATOR   FLIR ELECTRONICS   LASER

POWER SUPPLY   POD COMPUTER   FLIR SENSOR

CENTRAL ELECTRONICS   LASER ELECTRONICS   GIMBALLED MOUNT

ENVIRONMENTAL SYSTEM   LASER CONTROLLER

FUEL TANK

The Targeting Pod. A FLIR sensor and a laser fill the pod's nose. Turning up 35 degrees, down 235 degrees, and 6 degrees left or right, they allow the system to track a target while maneuvering. The pod's support equipment includes a boresight correlator, which shows the pilot the view a Maverick missile sees from its position far out under the wing.

control stick was set to release Sidewinders in case of MiG attack; with no interceptors in sight and the reactor just minutes away, he flicked a switch on the throttle to set the button for bomb release.

As the strike force approached the Euphrates River from the southwest, the F-15s gained altitude and formed a protective umbrella over the bombers, using their radar to scan for signs of MiGs taking off. Moments later, still hugging the deck, Raz caught sight of the reactor dome. Closing to a distance of four miles, he went to his afterburner for the pop-up. Stripped of more than half its fuel, the responsive Falcon soared to 5,000 feet in a few seconds. Then Raz rolled into his dive, going belly up briefly to avoid the unpleasant roller-coaster sensation as the plane started down and to keep the target in full view. As he righted himself, he lined up the reactor on his HUD so that the pipper was directly below the crown of the dome and moving toward it as the plane roared down. Though the script called for release at 4,000 feet, Raz waited an extra second for an added measure of accuracy and pickled off at 3,500. Pulling up and banking away, he saw both bombs drop through the dome, then felt the plane buck as the shock wave hit.

Falcon after Falcon swooped in with equal precision. Sixteen bombs fell within forty feet of each other—fifteen inside the dome—destroying the facility. The surprised defenders belatedly fired off AAA but failed to unleash a single SAM. The strike force beat a high-altitude retreat and returned unmolested to base with a little fuel to spare. A French technician had been killed in the raid, and even nations traditionally sympathetic to Israel criticized the operation. But privately, few states regretted the setback dealt to the nuclear program of an increasingly belligerent Iraqi regime.

Pulverizing the reactor demonstrated how effective low-level raids could be against opponents who were unprepared for the assault. But neither the United States nor its allies could hope to repeat such a coup once its adversaries were alert to the threat. Advanced SAMs available to the Iraqis and other Soviet clients by the 1970s did not rely solely on radar for guidance. The SA-9, for example, could be sighted optically and contained an infrared sensor that homed on the plane's heat. Moreover, it was small enough to be carried by a single soldier and fired from his shoulder. Or it could be mounted on a vehicle in groups of up to four and unleashed in a salvo. Defenders who anticipated an air strike against a vital target could bring in scores of these mobile SAMs and shoot down low-flying intruders even without radar warning of the attack. Such a defensive gambit would be much less effective at night, of course, but even then, attacking aircraft would be vulnerable when they popped up into radar range to get a fix on their target with infrared scopes. To strike with impunity, a plane would have to be a creature of the night and virtually invisible to radar.

By the early 1980s, the USAF was secretly trying out just such an intruder at the Tonopah Test Range in Nevada. Pilots recruited for the program were told that they would be flying venerable A-7 Corsair IIs, 1960s-vintage attack aircraft on the brink of retirement, to evaluate new avionics systems. Not until after a month of screening did they learn that they would actually be joining an elite unit, the 4450th Tactical Group, later to be designated the 37th Tactical Fighter Wing. The 4450th would be armed with a radical new aircraft—the F-117A stealth fighter, a plane whose angular features made it look so unstable skeptics dubbed it the Wobbly Goblin.

Sculpted with many facets to scatter radar signals and prevent the aircraft from appearing on enemy screens, the F-117 was further protected against detection by a coating of radar-absorbent material (RAM) and recessed engines whose exhaust was filtered and screened to frustrate heat-seeking SAMs (pages 69-75). Its twin turbofan engines sacrificed speed for endurance—the aircraft could not surpass mach 1, but it had a range of some 1,200 miles. Typically, the F-117 would attack after dark at an altitude of fifteen to twenty thousand feet, relying on recessed FLIR turrets that could pick out the target in the dark, magnify its image, and deliver a single 2,000-pound LGB on the mark; the plane could actually carry two such LGBs, but it would seldom expend both on the same objective. The nature of the F-117 and the small number built—the assembly line closed down after the fifty-ninth aircraft—meant that the stealth would normally be reserved for discrete, high-priority targets such as command-and-communications centers.

Learning to fly the F-117 was a bit unnerving. A simulator would not be available for many months, and there was no twin-seater version for training. So, after several dozen hours flying A-7s, which had similar flight characteristics, novices flew solo. And until November 1988, all flights, including maiden ones, were made at night to keep the plane a secret. The location of the cockpit—near the point of the V formed by the seamless junction of the delta wings with the tapered fuselage—did little to reassure the uninitiated. As one pilot remarked, "It feels like you're on the tip of a spear." But once launched and hurtling through the dark, the spear proved surprisingly stable. Equipped with fly-by-wire controls like the F-16, the Wobbly Goblin automatically compensated for any aerodynamic quirks in its design while remaining alert to the pilot's touch. The 4450th was certified combat-ready in October 1983. By that time, the pilots were calling themselves the Nighthawks.

Ironically, the F-117 first saw action against an opponent with no air defenses to speak of. When President George Bush decided in December 1989 to oust Panamanian dictator Manuel Noriega, the USAF, eager to demonstrate the plane, proposed using several stealth fighters to help neutralize the Panamanian Defense Force, Noriega's small army. The idea drew a skeptical response from Secretary of Defense Richard Cheney, who wondered why such aircraft were needed against a foe ill-equipped to detect and repulse conventional aircraft. Air Force chiefs explained that they wanted the F-117s in Panama for their precision and won approval for a plan that included an air strike by two of them, each to drop one 2,000-pound LGB in a field 150 meters from a barracks. The object was to shock the troops inside with blasts that one planner likened to "a giant stun grenade" and frighten them into submission.

As it turned out, the Panamanians had learned of the U.S. invasion in advance, lessening the impact of the raid. And fog around the barracks disrupted the laser targeting system, leading the first pilot to drop his bomb slightly farther from the barracks than planned; the second LGB fell in a dump perhaps 1,000 yards from the building. More than anything else, the mission pointed out that it is more difficult to miss a prominent structure precisely than to hit it.

Though no explanation could fully erase the chagrin felt by all concerned that the world's newest and most expensive fighter-bomber had been off target, pilots of the 37th Tactical Fighter Wing would not have to wait long for an opportunity to show what the stealth fighter could do. On August 19, 1990, just seventeen days after Iraqi troops invaded Kuwait, the first of the 37th's three squadrons was dispatched to Saudi Arabia. By January, almost the entire wing—forty-two F-117s in all—was stationed in the Persian Gulf. The men who flew at the tip of the spear were poised to strike deep into the Iraqi heartland.   ★

Regardless of color, shape, or size, no airplane is unobservable, especially at short range. Lit by the sun in the daytime and by the moon or antiaircraft artillery fire at night, each one can be seen, even if only fleetingly. Air that streams past its body and wings and surges through jet engines makes noise that can be heard on the ground. Moreover, the heat of combustion raises the aircraft's temperature, as does the friction caused as the plane parts the atmosphere. The resulting heat can be detected with infrared-sensing devices. And all aircraft, even those too far away to be seen or heard, are visible on radar, which can search farther than any human eye or infrared detector.

Because of these modes of detection, warplanes flying deep into enemy territory to strike well-defended targets must perform the near impossible: elude discovery by long-range radar and then run a gauntlet of sophisticated air-defense weapons that home on infrared radiation, are guided by radar, or are aimed by sight. It is a job in which losses are common. And yet during Operation Desert Wind, one aircraft—the F-117A stealth fighter shown below and on the following pages—not only flew such missions, it flew them repeatedly without suffering so much as a scratch.

A Radical Design for Nighttime Strikes

Like a Silent, Swift Arrow

The success enjoyed by the F-117A during the Persian Gulf War stemmed in part from the fact that the fighter is hard to see. Intended for night missions only, it is painted in light-absorbing black from nose to tail. Nothing is overlooked; even the ejection seat the pilot sits in and the helmet he wears are the color of night, and he looks through windows that have been coated to reduce glint. Fliers returning from the Gulf reported that the result was astonishing: When the fighter's external lights were switched off, the plane blended seamlessly into a darkened sky.

But there are other reasons for the F-117A's stealthiness. Its engines—ordinary nonafterburning turbofans similar to those on modern jetliners—have been constructed to quiet the roar from their exhaust nozzles. This helps make the fighter difficult to hear from a distance. Furthermore, the engines are positioned above the wing, deep within the body of the aircraft, where their exhaust is cooled to reduce its heat signature *(page 75)*, and the hot engine parts are hidden from view of ground-launched missiles that home on infrared radiation.

The largest factor in the F-117A's low profile, however, is the aircraft's ability to elude detection by radar. Even though the plane's wingspan exceeds forty-three feet and its length approaches sixty-six feet, the F-117A reflects about the same amount of radar energy as a hummingbird—a characteristic caused by several unusual features. Shape is one. The stealth fighter was de-

A BLACK JEWEL. An F-117A will likely meet the first hostile radar signals head-on. To parry them, the wing's leading edge is ruler straight and swept back at an angle of sixty-seven degrees. It deflects such waves sideways and rearward, not forward. Signals coming from other bearings are deflected by the fighter's flat surface panels. Tilted at least thirty degrees from vertical, they send most reflections upward, not directly back to the radar.

signed so that none of its sloping surfaces form right angles, which make ideal reflectors of radar waves. For instance, the fuselage and wings, rather than meeting at ninety degrees, are blended into a pyramid shape. Two outward-slanting fins—not a traditional vertical and horizontal stabilizer—serve as its tail. And unlike other attack aircraft, the F-117A carries all munitions and fuel internally, instead of on pylons that hang under the wings or fuselage.

The F-117A is also atypical in that its shape is composed of flat, straight-edged panels, rather than the smooth, curving skin found on more recent stealth aircraft, the B-2 bomber and the advanced tactical fighter. When the F-117A was designed, in the 1970s, computer software had not been developed that could help engineers create curved surfaces that do not reflect radar waves back toward the transmitter. The radar characteristics of two-dimensional surfaces, however, could be calculated more

PROTECTED INLETS. The F-117A's engines are buried within its body at the end of air ducts whose inlets are covered with rectangular grids *(below)*. Made of intersecting knife-edged blades and coated with radar-absorbing material, the grids keep most incoming waves from reaching the turbofans, which make excellent radar reflectors.

ONE-WAY GLASS. The glass in the five flat canopy windows is made with a laminate that allows the pilot to look out but prevents radar waves from entering the cockpit and bouncing off unstealthy items inside. Without the coating, the reflection from the pilot's helmet, for instance, would be greater than that from the entire aircraft.

SAWTOOTH EDGES. Any seam or ridge that runs perpendicular to the path of a radar wave will reflect the wave directly toward the sender. On the F-117A, the forward edges of the windows, the canopy, and the five-sided bay above the nose all cause such reflections, but because the lines are jagged, they send the signals to the left and right, away from the radar.

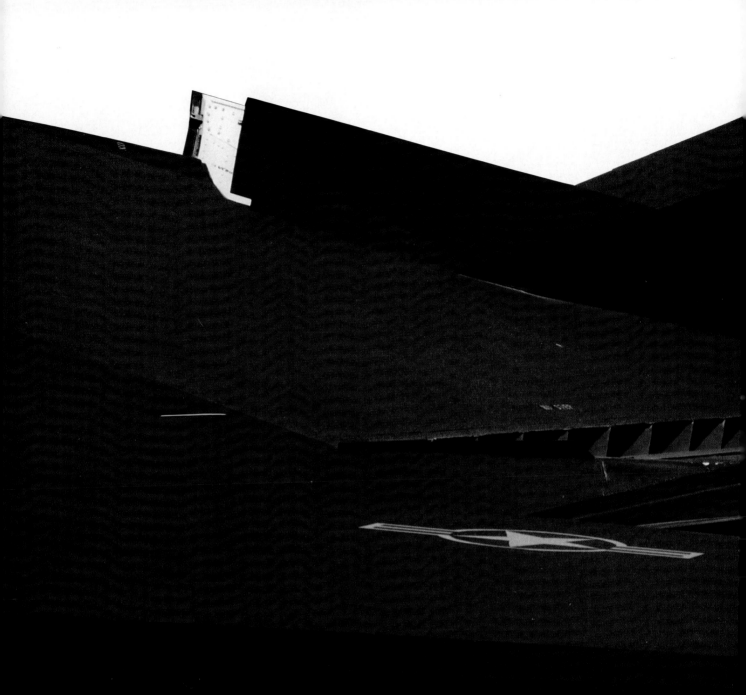

easily; they reflect incoming waves as flat mirrors do. Unless such a surface is perpendicular to the signal's path, it will not return an echo to the sender.

In most aircraft, seams in the skin cause strong radar echoes. Skin panels for the F-117A, however, are precisely machined and placed on the plane's aluminum-alloy skeleton so that they lie only a ten-thousandth of an inch apart—close enough to make the seams virtually invisible to radar. Those that cannot be made so fine—the seam between the canopy and the fuselage, for example—receive special treatment *(page 73)*.

After assembly, the entire aircraft is mounted in a huge custom-made fixture and rotated while computer-controlled nozzles spray it with a paint that absorbs radar energy. The formula is secret.

Areas of the fighter that are especially likely to produce strong radar echoes, such as the air ducts on either side of the fuselage, are lined with other radar-absorbent material. Windows for the infrared sensors in the nose and under the cockpit are covered with radar-absorbing mesh, like that found in the doors of microwave ovens, to prevent radar waves from reaching reflective components on the other side. The canopy glass gets similar treatment *(page 72)*.

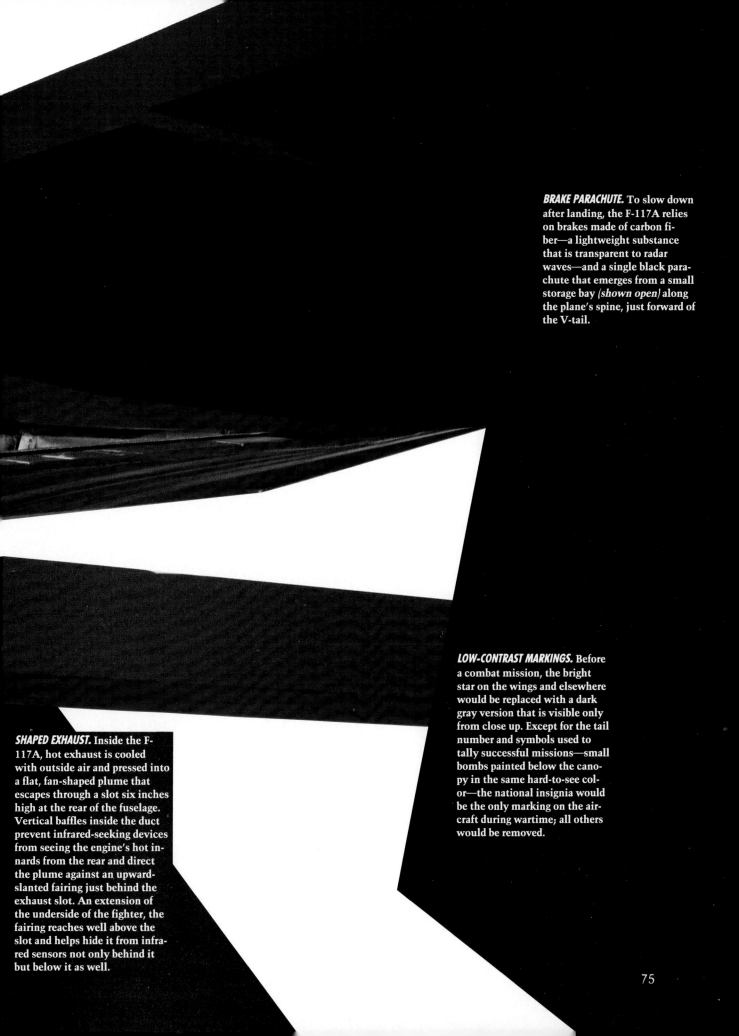

BRAKE PARACHUTE. To slow down after landing, the F-117A relies on brakes made of carbon fiber—a lightweight substance that is transparent to radar waves—and a single black parachute that emerges from a small storage bay *(shown open)* along the plane's spine, just forward of the V-tail.

LOW-CONTRAST MARKINGS. Before a combat mission, the bright star on the wings and elsewhere would be replaced with a dark gray version that is visible only from close up. Except for the tail number and symbols used to tally successful missions—small bombs painted below the canopy in the same hard-to-see color—the national insignia would be the only marking on the aircraft during wartime; all others would be removed.

SHAPED EXHAUST. Inside the F-117A, hot exhaust is cooled with outside air and pressed into a flat, fan-shaped plume that escapes through a slot six inches high at the rear of the fuselage. Vertical baffles inside the duct prevent infrared-seeking devices from seeing the engine's hot innards from the rear and direct the plume against an upward-slanted fairing just behind the exhaust slot. An extension of the underside of the fighter, the fairing reaches well above the slot and helps hide it from infrared sensors not only behind it but below it as well.

The Howling Wind of Desert Storm

Thundering into the Saudi Arabian sky on full afterburner, an F-15E Strike Eagle—one of forty-eight deployed for Operation Desert Wind—carries a lethal load of twelve cluster-bomb canisters, plus four Sidewinder air-to-air missiles and a centerline fuel tank. The F-15Es flew night and day, hitting every kind of target, from Iraqi radar sites to tanks hiding in the desert.

Seen through satellite eyes in the early-morning hours of January 17, 1991, Iraq was a land asleep. Wisps of clouds drifted across its dim expanses. The roads were quiet, the cities somnolent. But an insectile babble of pulses from air-defense radars told of the nation's alertness to the dangers of the night. Less than twenty-four hours earlier, the UN deadline for the withdrawal of Iraqi forces from Kuwait had passed. Now Saddam Hussein waited. He waited with an army approaching a million men, more than 3,000 artillery pieces, better than 5,000 tanks, almost 1,000 aircraft, as many as 17,000 surface-to-air missiles, perhaps 10,000 antiaircraft guns, and tightly woven systems for the control and supply of this vast military apparatus.

To the south, other forces were stirring. Throughout the night, airmen in Saudi Arabia, in the Arab emirates, and on aircraft carriers stationed in the Persian Gulf and the Red Sea had been studying their lines in a highly detailed script—the Air Tasking Order, or ATO—generated at the Tactical Air Control Center in the Saudi city of Riyadh. Based on five months of intelligence gathering, it listed about a hundred targets that would be hit by coalition aircraft in the hours ahead: command centers, communications facilities, radar installations, airfields, power-generation plants, production and storage sites for chemical weapons, laboratories for the development of nuclear weapons—and many more. The document assigned radio frequencies, call signs, and altitudes to the attacking aircraft; the moment bombs were to detonate; the type of plane to be used; times and places for refueling; and other mission details. Given the scope and weight of the assault, the choreography had to be exact. "We were totally integrated," said Brigadier General Buster G. Glosson, one of the principal tacticians. "We knew which airplane would be most successful against a specific target, and we used the system to get the maximum we could out of each plane."

But detailed plans extended far beyond this night. Air commanders had plotted out weeks of bombing, a round-the-clock campaign named Desert Wind. The offensive would have four basic purposes: to dismember the Iraqi air-defense system and the nexus of resources that military planners called C cubed I, or C^3I—for command, control, communications, and intelligence; to shut off supplies to Iraq's huge ground army; to soften up that army by direct attacks; and, last, to provide close air support during a ground war if, as many expected, bombardment alone could not dislodge Saddam Hussein from Kuwait. Except for the final installment of the campaign, these air-war phases, as planners termed them, would overlap. There would be no respite or refuge for the enemy. Forty-three days and nights of devastation lay ahead.

The raising of the hammer on January 17 began with combat-support aircraft. Four big AWACS planes were in the air by midnight, orbiting well south of the Iraqi border. Fitted with banks of computers and powerful radars capable of detecting aerial activity up to 300 miles away, they would serve as the eyes of the attack force, watching for hostile aircraft and directing traffic in the skies. At about 1:00 a.m., sixty tankers—airborne gas stations—assumed their posts in the sky. Carrying as much as 200,000 pounds of fuel apiece, they would top off the tanks of the strike aircraft before they headed into Iraq and give them another drink when they returned.

With this support in place, combat aircraft roared aloft from air bases and carriers, leaping into the blackness at the rate of one every few seconds, radios silent, gathering in groups and circling as they awaited the go-ahead. The swirling assemblage—a monstrous hurricane building above the desert sands—was diverse in makeup. In the first wave, some twenty U.S. Air Force F-15C Eagle air-to-air fighters had the job of dealing with any Iraqi interceptors that might rise to meet the strike aircraft. A contingent of EF-111 Ravens was assigned to jam Iraqi radars. Wild Weasels in the form of F-4G Phantoms carried missiles that would home on radars and destroy them. And then there were the planes that would deliver the bulk of the bombs: F-15Es, swing-wing F-111F Aardvark fighter-bombers, Navy and Marine Corps A-6Es, as well as British and Saudi Tornadoes. About 200 of these fighter-bombers—some in flights of four or six and others grouped, along with fighter escorts and the antiradar specialists, into strike packages of thirty to sixty aircraft—would take part in this initial assault. Subsequent waves would include F-16 Falcons, F/A-18 Hornets, French Jaguars, and even Kuwaiti A-4 Skyhawks—some twenty-five different types of aircraft from seven nations in all.

There was also a strange newcomer, an angular, black, batlike craft, bred for darkness and resembling something out of another age—the deep past or far future. This was the F-117A stealth fighter, so difficult to detect by radar that it had been assigned to fly, unescorted by jammers or F-15s, to the very center of Saddam Hussein's web. Some fifteen of these stealth fighters led the first wave.

Nor was that all. From the sea would come a weapon that had never before been used in combat. It made its debut about 1:30 a.m., when a fire-control officer on the guided-missile cruiser *San Jacinto*, stationed in the Red Sea, pushed a black button marked "Execute." Within an armored box, a rocket booster roared, pushing the snout of an eighteen-foot-long Tomahawk cruise missile through the rubbery membrane sealing its launch tube.

Spewing yellow flames for about twelve seconds, the booster lifted the missile out over the water, where it hung crazily in the air for an instant as stubby wings popped out and a turbojet engine whined to life. The $1.3-million missile then headed off toward the coastline at better than 500 miles per hour, guided by its inertial navigation system. Once over land, skimming close to the ground to avoid radar, it would find its unerring way by consulting programmed memories of terrain elevations and the appearance of the target *(pages 85-87)*. The *San Jacinto* was not alone in firing these drone weapons. A sister cruiser, the USS *Bunker Hill*, fired the first Tomahawk from the Persian Gulf. Moments later, the battleships *Wisconsin* and *Missouri* joined in.

In the opening salvo, nine ships dispatched fifty-one Tomahawks toward heavily defended targets in Iraq (a fifty-second failed to leave the launcher). The loss of a cruise missile could be contemplated with equanimity, but piloted aircraft were an altogether different matter, a life-or-death issue that planners had pondered deeply. Airmen would be entering an environment potentially more deadly than any ever encountered in the history of warfare—a world guarded by advanced MiG and Mirage fighters, by masses of antiaircraft artillery effective to altitudes of about 20,000 feet, and by surface-to-air missiles that could reach as high as 70,000 feet. These defenses depended heavily on ground-based radar to spot the enemy and direct the planes, missiles, or guns toward a kill. The Iraqis had "very modern radars," General Merrill McPeak, U.S. Air Force Chief of Staff, would later say, "all lashed together with high-tech equipment—lots of computer data links, fiberoptic connections, many of the principal control nodes hardened. A first-class air defense."

For the F-117s, no more visible to radar than a hummingbird, the air-defense system could be largely ignored. These ghostly craft slipped into Iraqi air space unnoticed around 2:30 a.m. But the orbiting armada of conventional planes hung back, lurking below the beams of groping search radars. Two early-warning radar installations were of particular concern. They lay near Iraq's southern border, athwart the route that the attackers would have to take into the country. These electronic eyes would have to be blinded.

An Assist from the Army

At 2:38 a.m., eight Apache helicopters of the 101st Airborne Division swept across the border. Hugging the ground, they approached to within four miles of the radar sites and fired Hellfire missiles. One of the pilots—his voice tape-recorded—offered a kind of invocation: "This one's for you, Saddam." Onto each target, the Apaches beamed laser light for sensors in the noses of the missiles to home on. Lancing toward these laser beacons at supersonic speed, the missiles first blasted electrical generators. Deprived of power, the radars instantly went off the air. Then, using additional Hellfires and their 30-mm automatic cannons, the Apache gunners systematically demolished the radar antennas and support buildings.

Anticipating the destruction of these radars, the coalition armada surged toward Iraq in a great wave, the EF-111s and Wild Weasels racing in front to wage their electronic warfare, the F-15Cs flying escort, the fighter-bombers hurtling toward their targets. Ahead, the Apaches' action unfolded almost cinematically. Said Captain Mark Alred, an F-15E pilot: "As we approached this one radar, about twenty-five miles from it, I watched the thing blow up in front of me." It was still burning as he howled past at 500 miles per hour toward a target thirty minutes away. For the first time, he realized just how carefully coordinated this night's activities would be.

An E-3 Sentry AWACS (for airborne warning and control system) keeps watch on Iraq with its thirty-foot rotating radar dome. Inside, sixteen console operators, each responsible for a sector of air space, could track as many as 600 planes at distances up to 300 miles. A typical mission lasted fifteen hours, so these nerve centers carried two shifts of controllers.

As the first gusts of Desert Wind rolled into Iraq, the AWACS kept the escort fighters informed of the locations of enemy planes in the air. From previously developed intelligence associating airfields, call signs, and electronic identification codes with different types of Iraqi aircraft, the planes could even tell which planes the enemy sent aloft. The four AWACS also fed all of their data to the Tactical Air Control Center in Riyadh. On a pair of giant radar screens there, the hundreds of planes involved in the assault appeared as blinking flecks of light. "Time kind of stood still as you saw those little dots moving toward Iraq," remembered one witness of the scene. But any sense of satisfaction at what was about to befall Saddam Hussein's military empire was shadowed by the somber expectation that men would lose their lives that night.

Trouble arrived in a hurry. Some of the EF-111 Ravens in the vanguard were met by MiG-29 Fulcrums and MiG-25 Foxbats. The unarmed jamming planes dived for the deck and used their terrain-following radar computers to race at high speed just 200 feet above the landscape. The Iraqi fighters fired missiles at them, but losing their targets in a deluge of radar echoes from the ground, they slammed to earth behind the sprinting Ravens.

The first air-to-air kill occurred near Baghdad. Captain Steve Tate, leader of four F-15Cs flying combat air patrol, received a report from an E-3 AWACS that an F-1 Mirage was chasing his number three. The F-15s were split into flights of two, flying stacked race-track patterns so that one pair of fighters always faced Iraq and the potential threat. Thus, Tate was flying in the general direction of the approaching Mirage, while the other flight was heading away. Turning toward the threat, he locked his fire-control radar onto the bandit, which he could identify on his radar; hostile blips appeared as a different shape than friendly ones. At a range of twelve miles, he loosed an AIM-7 Sparrow missile. It left the rails with a whoosh audible in the cockpit and a blinding light from the rocket-engine exhaust, which winked out twenty seconds later as the missile exhausted its fuel. Then a fireball bloomed in the darkness.

By then, Iraq was a maelstrom of missiles, bombs, swirling planes, and antiaircraft fire. But the response of the enemy fighters, SAMs, and antiaircraft guns was a panicked flailing. Iraqi guidance radars on the ground were being swamped by a torrent of high-energy jamming by EF-111s flying irregular patterns in the sky.

At the same time, the Wild Weasels were on the prowl. The F-4Gs

knew exactly what they were looking for: Months of reconnaissance had revealed to coalition planners the locations and frequencies of key radars. Detecting telltale frequencies, the Wild Weasels launched HARM missiles that rode right down the beams at twice the speed of sound and shattered the radars with a lethal spray of 25,000 corn-kernel-size steel cubes. Many radar operators, realizing that they were attracting a killer, blinked their beams on and off—which seriously degraded radar performance—or shut them down altogether. As a result, the Iraqi planes were left to search for the enemy on their own; missiles were flung into the sky without guidance; and antiaircraft guns sprayed wildly at a threat that seemed everywhere and nowhere. In southern Iraq, for example, a SAM battery fired an unguided fusillade of six Vietnam-era SA-2s at a Wild Weasel—probably upon hearing the F-4 overhead—on the slim chance that one of them would pass close to the aircraft and trip a proximity fuze in one of the missiles. Alerted by the brilliant glow from the missiles' rocket motors, the pilot yanked his plane into a five-G turn away from the SAMs.

Behind the electronic warriors came the fighter-bombers, focusing on airfields, command posts, and communications centers. On this night, the aim was to deal a disabling blow to what planners described as the "brain and nervous system" of the Iraqi military, leaving its forces confused, uncoordinated, floundering. That collective goal included shattering the Iraqi Air Force, which, in addition to its offensive and defensive roles, was Iraq's chief means of gath-

Crammed with electronic gear to locate and identify enemy air-defense radars, F-4G Wild Weasels cleared the way for fighter-bombers by launching HARM missiles that homed on the emissions and shredded the radar equipment with fragmentation warheads. To take advantage of their nearly sixteen-mile range, the missiles could be programmed to hunt for ground radars on their own after being launched toward a likely area.

ering intelligence on coalition activities in Saudi Arabia, the Persian Gulf, and other areas. Without aerial reconnaissance, Saddam Hussein and his commanders could have no real comprehension of enemy moves—and thus no notion of how to counter them.

The aerial hammer fell all across Iraq, but nowhere more heavily than on Baghdad. This was the center, the locus of decision making, the proud national bastion that had scarcely been touched in the course of the eight-year war with Iran. Few places on earth possessed such extensive and sophisticated air defenses—or were better suited to attack by cruise missiles.

Out of the night, flying low and unseen along programmed paths, came the swarm of Tomahawks launched an hour or so earlier from the Persian Gulf and the Red Sea, each missile packing 1,000 pounds of high explosive in its forebody. As they began striking radar sites, command centers, power-generation yards, SAM batteries, and other vital targets, the city erupted in an immense, reflexive spasm of antiaircraft fire, filling the sky with tracers. It was in vain. Sheets of flame flashed around the skyline as, one after the other, the missiles hit home.

Just before 3:00 a.m., Baghdad went black. Lieutenant General Charles Horner, commander of coalition air forces, would later explain: "We hit the electrical production to invoke hardship on military command and control, to stress it. But there's no doubt that was a reminder that Saddam Hussein was conducting a war in the south and was unable to contain it."

Target for Tonight — Baghdad

The F-117s arrived almost simultaneously with the blackout, and they came alone. Planners had concluded that the stealth fighters were the only type of plane with any great chance of surviving unescorted over Baghdad that night; no other piloted aircraft would venture within the city limits during the entire war. The F-117s were flown by the Air Force's most experienced fighter pilots, several years older than the average combat pilot and highly trained in their night-bombing specialty. Each aircraft carried two 2,000-pound laser-guided bombs. Fourteen feet long, they were steered by the movable vanes of a laser-seeking "guidance kit" on the nose.

En route to the tanker to top off their fuel tanks, the planes flew

The Tomahawk cruise missile *(left)* and similar weapons are direct descendants of Nazi Germany's V-1s, the infamous buzz bombs that terrorized England late in World War II. But while a V-1 was lucky to hit a target the size of London from 300 miles away, a Tomahawk can strike a specific individual building—or even a particular floor of that building—after a flight of 1,500 miles. This phenomenal leap in accuracy is the result of computer-controlled, radar-assisted navigation.

At the heart of the matter lies an inertial navigation system (INS), an assembly of gyroscopes and sensors that calculates airspeed and heading. But even a highly advanced INS produces minuscule errors that can compound to put the missile wide of the target by several miles after a 1,500-mile flight. To prevent this, the Tomahawk's computer makes midcourse corrections using two kinds of maps based on information gathered by satellites.

The first is called a terrain contour matching (TERCOM) map. It employs elevation data to check on the missile's progress and correct its course. The second type is photographic; it is used by a device called a digital scene matching correlator (DSMAC). With the help of TERCOM and DSMAC, planners can put the Tomahawk on target with an error estimated at no more than twenty feet.

A Tomahawk leaps skyward, propelled by its booster rocket. After the missile clears the launcher, stubby wings and tail fins pop out, the booster falls away, and the Tomahawk's turbofan jet engine takes over.

In the hypothetical mission illustrated below, the INS guides the Tomahawk from launch to landfall *(left of diagram)*, bringing it to the first TERCOM map, a large grid of squares called cells. Mission programmers assign each cell a numerical value based on the average elevation of the terrain within it, thus creating a digital contour map that can be stored in the Tomahawk's computer memory.

As the missile nears the coast, it descends and activates a radar altimeter that measures the height of the missile above the ground. An average of such readings, subtracted from the missile's height above sea level, gives a number like those stored in the computer. Any path across the TERCOM map *(purple ribbon)* yields a sequence of numbers that, when compared with the elevations in memory, reveals the course flown by the missile. If necessary, the TERCOM system issues a course correction to return to the projected track *(yellow ribbon)*. In this case, the missile jinks left, then right. From INS variances, the computer learns of any bias inherent in the system and compensates during the next leg.

Since TERCOM relies on variations in elevation, mission planners seek out distinctive terrain for their maps. Here, the preplanned flight path turns right, then left, so that the next map can use the contours of a river valley. After clearing the

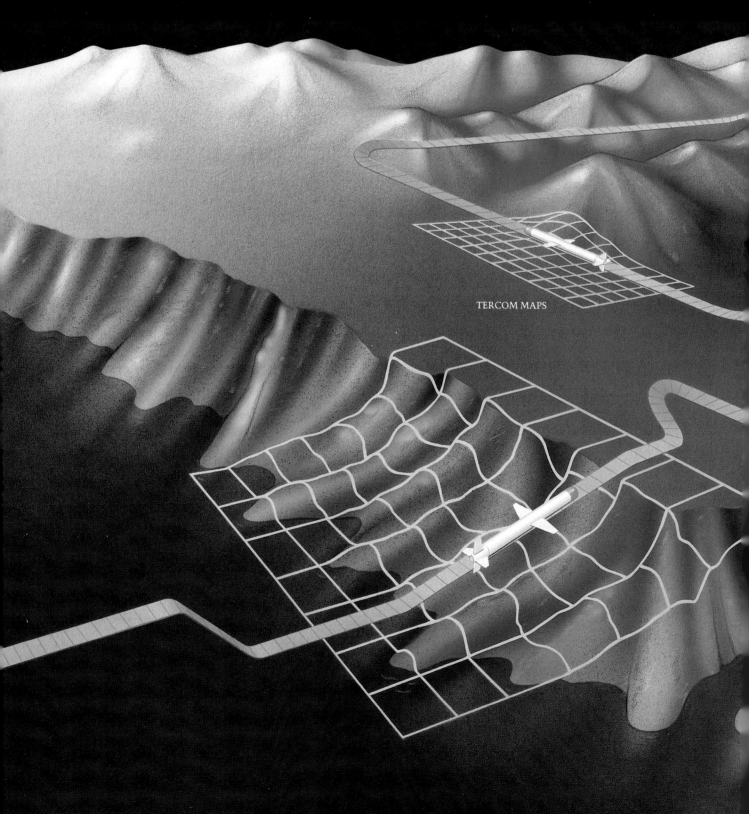

TERCOM MAPS

second map, which has smaller cells than the first, the Tomahawk refines its compensation for INS bias and executes a hard left turn, beginning a long, roundabout path to its destination. This route will confuse ground observers as to the target, bypass a SAM site, and avoid the flat, featureless landscape that makes a direct approach unsuitable to TERCOM.

Succeeding maps—and their cells—become progressively smaller as bias compensation becomes more precise. The final TERCOM map ensures impact within about forty feet of the aiming point, astonishing but still not sufficient to hit a small target. To further refine accuracy, DSMAC comes into play.

Instead of elevations, DSMAC works with patterns of light and dark. Satellite photographs are divided into cells, representing squares of ground as small as ten feet on a side. Each cell is stored in the computer as an image in two shades of gray. Upon nearing the target, the computer turns on a downward-scanning video camera (at night, a strobe

illuminates the scene) and begins to look for a match with the first of several DSMAC maps. Upon finding a correlation, the Tomahawk arms itself, and final course adjustments are made as the missile crosses succeeding maps. Then, the Tomahawk either plows straight into the target or pops up at the last moment to strike from above.

DSMAC MAPS

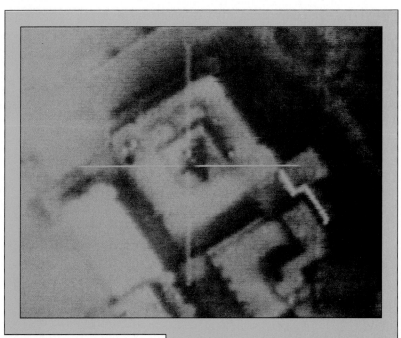

in pairs with their flashing position lights on. But after refueling, lights were extinguished and each stealth fighter struck out on its own, even when two aircraft were assigned the same target to be sure it was destroyed. Occasionally, F-117 pilots—as well as other airmen abroad that night—distracted themselves with rock-and-roll or country music, slipping the earplugs of cassette players beneath their headsets as they flew toward enemy territory. Others said prayers—aloud sometimes, and later audible on tapes from a cockpit recorder activated when the pilot switched on the plane's targeting system—as they approached a well-defended area.

In one of many surgically exact blows delivered in downtown Baghdad on the opening night of Desert Wind, a laser-guided 2,000-pound bomb from an F-117A fighter-bomber plunges into an air ventilation shaft of the Iraqi Air Force headquarters just before blowing the building apart from within. Once a stealth pilot took aim with the cross hairs of his infrared targeting system, a laser beam automatically held on the designated spot until the bomb struck home. During the first hours of the war, the F-117s slipped through massive Iraqi defenses to hit nearly forty critical targets.

One F-117 pilot assigned to Baghdad told of seeing in the distance an orange radiance that reminded him of the glow of charcoal in a barbecue. A quick check of the map told him the sight could only be the Iraqi capital. "That's Baghdad," Captain Terry Foley muttered to himself, "but what's going on?" As he neared the city, Foley understood what he was seeing. "Oh my God," he said, "that's triple-A, it's nothing but triple-A." From a distance, tracks of individual tracers had fused into a singular glow.

In order not to be distracted by the awful vision outside, he lowered his seat (it is adjustable to accommodate pilots of different heights) and flew his plane entirely by instruments. From time to time, however, he could not resist peeking over the cockpit rail as he flew closer to the cauldron of groundfire. "God," he would say when a missile or cannon shells happened to pass or explode nearby, "just please let me survive this." Despite the terror of the approach, Foley became very businesslike when the moment came to bomb his target, a command-and-control facility. He scored a direct hit.

Another F-117 headed for Baghdad's communications hub, a multistory building on the east bank of the Tigris River. As though in slow motion, the structure slid into view on a screen in the cockpit, rendered with near-daytime clarity by an infrared sensor producing a television-like image. By means of cross hairs on the screen, the pilot positioned the laser beam on a microwave tower atop the building and pressed a button, indicating to the plane's fire-control computer that the tower was where he wanted the bomb to strike. The computer, in turn, told the pilot when to pickle off the bomb. Upon release, the huge weapon steered its way toward the laser's call—and hit right on the money. Chunks of concrete flew in all directions as all four sides of the building blew outward. When the smoke cleared, the top floors had been demolished.

Elsewhere, F-117s hit microwave repeating stations, radar installations, and underground command bunkers. A stealth pilot put a bomb through the skylight of one of Saddam's residences. Another bomb penetrated the roof of the multistory headquarters of the Iraqi Air Force, exploding within. Still another entered the air-defense headquarters by way of an air shaft in the roof, blowing the building's doors outward. For some hardened targets, the F-117s punched a hole in reinforced concrete, then sent a second bomb down the hole to complete the destruction. It was an unprecedented demonstration of bombing accuracy, impressive even to those who carried it out. Later, Colonel Alton Whitley, commander of the 37th TFW, said, "I saw a lot of old boys become young men last night."

When Foley completed his bombing run, he knew in his heart that the wing must have "lost three or four airplanes, somebody has to have gotten shot down." He kept count as his squadronmates checked in by radio after exiting Iraq and, miracle of miracles, no one was missing. After landing, he grabbed a flashlight to examine his plane, expecting to see it peppered with shrapnel holes. He and his crew chief scrutinized the plane closely, but could find not a mark on it. No F-117 was hit by antiaircraft fire that night.

Throughout the war, the stealth aircraft would remain untouched, though not entirely undetected by radar. F-117 pilot Major Jon Boyd, while cruising toward Baghdad, became aware of an aircraft nearby flying with its lights on. At first he thought it might be an F-15 whose pilot had forgotten to extinguish them, but that explanation seemed unlikely when the plane began to shadow his course—now heading away, now returning, as if receiving not quite enough guidance to find the F-117. Boyd decided the plane was Iraqi, flying all lit up perhaps to avoid being shot at by his own air defenses. For the half hour the aircraft tried to follow him, Boyd said later, "I was just watching him, waiting to react in case he came after me, but he never did. It's sort of like playing blindman's buff with live munitions, so you try to get through a room of these people. They're trying to find you, but they can't."

The stealth planes were not reserved only for Baghdad. They struck at many points across the country—wherever a target was particularly critical and the defenses especially formidable. In a number of cases, F-117s went in just a few minutes ahead of conventional fighter-bombers to take out air-defense radar, then proceeded to another target as F-15Es or F-111s followed with their own rain of laser- and TV-guided bombs. In all, the F-117s hit 31 percent of the targets listed in the opening-night script, even though they represented only about two percent of the aircraft sent into Iraq and Kuwait in those first raging hours of Desert Wind.

Aardvarks on the Rampage

The northernmost strikes were carried out by a flight of six F-111Fs led by Colonel Tom Lennon, commander of the 48th Tactical Fighter Wing. Their initial target was a major military airfield at Balad, about fifty miles northwest of Baghdad. Lennon and his wingman had been assigned to hit a large hangar and the airfield's control tower with optically guided bombs; the other four planes were to

On the runway of a Saudi air base, munitions specialists ready an F-16C for a mission, uncovering the seeker heads of the wing-tip Sidewinder missiles and pulling out pins to arm the plane's 20-mm gun and a pair of 2,000-pound bombs, which are carried outboard of underwing fuel tanks.

drop mines on both ends of the runway and around aircraft shelters. These planes would be in the air for about six and a half hours.

Some improvisation was required early on. The plan called for the F-111s to fly about 130 miles into Iraq at an altitude of several thousand feet. But forty-five miles inside the border, their warning systems detected an SA-2 radar looking at them. They descended to 750 feet to thwart the SAM system, then went to 400 feet as they crossed the Euphrates near Baghdad. An Iraqi fighter—hunting with its lights on—appeared on the left. The F-111s dropped to 200 feet, accelerated to 600 knots, and left it in their dust.

About twenty miles from the target, they began climbing in preparation for lofting a bomb toward the target. The sky ahead reddened with AAA fire. Expecting an attack, airfield defenders were taking no chances. Seven miles from the airfield, as the F-1i1 reached 5,000 feet, Lennon pickled off the bomb—which failed to release. Now in the midst of heavy barrage fire, Lennon veered away. "As we turned the corner," he later said, "the triple-A actually started following us as if it was tracking the sound. It didn't seem to be looking at us with radar." His wingman got off his bomb unmolested about a minute and a half later. Then Lennon, completing his turn, came right back down the original corridor of attack, allowing his WSO, Captain Steve Williams, to put a bomb through the door of the hangar. Clouds of dust from the pulverized buildings drifted across the airfield. At ninety-second intervals, the four other planes swooped in and released more than 1,500 mines that would make the runway and taxiways unusable for hours.

Next, Lennon and his wingman headed off to hit Saddam Hussein's summer palace, about forty miles north of the airfield. This target, too, proved well defended. As Williams held the plane's laser beam on the structure, three French-made Roland missiles darted upward. Lennon maneuvered to evade them, but doing so took him through a heavy barrage of AAA fire. Unhit, he then dodged a Soviet-made SAM by turning toward it and diving earthward, leveling out at 200 feet. From that point on, Lennon stayed on the deck and, as he put it, "exited about as fast as we could."

For this attack, the F-111s had followed each other straight into the target. Later, however, tactics would be altered to resemble an airshow maneuver called the bomb burst, in which planes barrel toward each other at high speed from different points of the compass, relying on timing and altitude discipline to avoid a collision as they cross. Airshow pilots performing this stunt have two advantages: They can see each other and talk on the radio. The F-111 pilots, flying at night over hostile territory, could do neither. The planes approached a target one behind the other, spaced so that they would reach preselected turning points surrounding the objective at times that would allow them to attack it from four or five directions simultaneously. The object was to prevent defenders from using the first plane's axis of attack to predict the approach of others and thereby refine their aim. By the end of the war, experience would reduce the interval between planes to less than a minute.

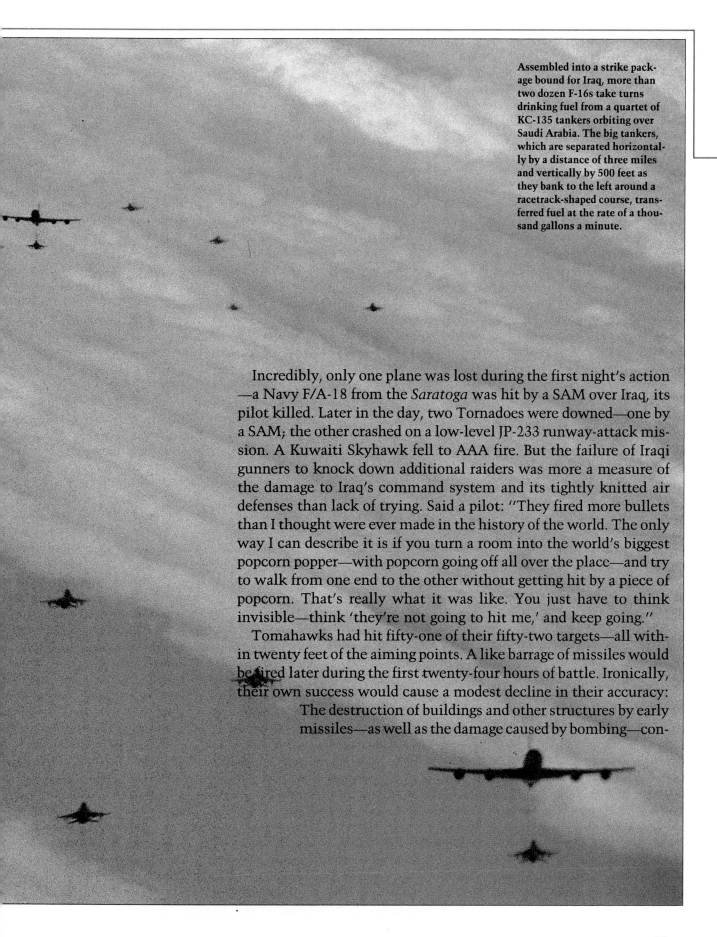

Incredibly, only one plane was lost during the first night's action —a Navy F/A-18 from the *Saratoga* was hit by a SAM over Iraq, its pilot killed. Later in the day, two Tornadoes were downed—one by a SAM; the other crashed on a low-level JP-233 runway-attack mission. A Kuwaiti Skyhawk fell to AAA fire. But the failure of Iraqi gunners to knock down additional raiders was more a measure of the damage to Iraq's command system and its tightly knitted air defenses than lack of trying. Said a pilot: "They fired more bullets than I thought were ever made in the history of the world. The only way I can describe it is if you turn a room into the world's biggest popcorn popper—with popcorn going off all over the place—and try to walk from one end to the other without getting hit by a piece of popcorn. That's really what it was like. You just have to think invisible—think 'they're not going to hit me,' and keep going."

Tomahawks had hit fifty-one of their fifty-two targets—all within twenty feet of the aiming points. A like barrage of missiles would be fired later during the first twenty-four hours of battle. Ironically, their own success would cause a modest decline in their accuracy: The destruction of buildings and other structures by early missiles—as well as the damage caused by bombing—con-

Except for a suddenly useless transmission tower, only rubble remains of a communications center in Baghdad after a visit by stealth fighters early in the war. Destruction of communications nodes at the outset of the air campaign not only threw the Iraqi command-and-control system into disarray but also sent an unmistakable message of coalition potency to the population at large.

fused the scene-matching guidance systems of some that followed.

General Horner later said of Saddam's military machine, "We wanted to seize the initiative immediately. In the first ten minutes of the war, we wanted to shock him and paralyze him." To a degree he had hardly dared hope for, the coalition armada had done just that. Iraq was reeling, stunned by a blow delivered with supreme efficiency. Horner's chief planner, General Glosson, added: "We've always looked at warfare as being speed, mass, and surprise. I believe we've changed that forever to speed, precision, and surprise."

Radio Baghdad offered its own skewed version of what was happening in the air war. After the first day, the government reported that forty-four coalition aircraft had been shot down and that—by an unexplained means—twenty-three cruise missiles had been recovered. The country's Revolutionary Command Council "praised the capability of our armed forces for confronting the American and Zionist aggression and inflicting huge casualties on them. It is a day of holy struggle against the infidels."

Even before the first strike planes had returned to base, more aircraft were heading into Iraq to hit airfields; military headquarters; power plants; facilities related to chemical, biological, and nuclear weapons; communications nodes; and other targets. More than a thousand sorties would be flown in the first fourteen hours of the war, and the sortie total would mount to almost 1,400 by day's end. British, French, Saudi, Italian, Canadian, and Kuwaiti aircraft all took part, although the United States carried the heaviest load. A Wild Weasel pilot captured the exhilaration felt by many: "It was probably the most exciting day of my life."

But the work was just beginning, and the strategic phases of the air campaign would continue for days and weeks, as coalition air forces steadily whittled away at Iraq's ability to make war.

A Mirage of an Air Force

From the outset of the air campaign, when a few interceptors rose to meet coalition planes, the efforts of Iraq's fighter pilots were halfhearted and erratic. U.S. Navy aviators who flew a daytime attack on an airfield in southwestern Iraq recounted that a group of MiGs kept at least forty miles away, retreating each time the American planes made a move in their direction. Farther north Iraqi

fighters zigzagged between two sets of coalition aircraft. The leader of an A-7 attack squadron recounted, "They acted as if they were overwhelmed by the numbers of aircraft coming toward them and they couldn't quite make up their mind which strike group to go after. We expected them to have fighter aircraft more regimented, more uniform in their attack, but they were truly random."

On another occasion, two MiG-29 Fulcrums (the Soviet Union's most advanced fighter) dared to approach a sixty-plane strike package of F-15 escorts, EF-111 jammers, Wild Weasels, and two dozen F-16 fighter-bombers. Alerted by an AWACS crew, the F-15 MiGCAP launched a pair of Sparrow missiles, blasting the MiGs from the sky. Within hours of the first air strikes, elements of the beleaguered Iraqi Air Force began to move to the northern parts of the country, in order to be as far as possible from the bases and carriers launching aircraft toward them. But refuge there would be short-lived. On the first day of battle, the parliament of Turkey voted to allow U.S. planes to fight from a base in that country, putting northern Iraqi airfields within easy reach.

As Desert Wind gained momentum, the number of missions steadily increased, ratcheting up toward the wartime average of more than 2,500 sorties per day, flown by a combined force of nearly 2,800 aircraft of all types. The coordination of this stupendous air assault was a huge job, made possible only by a unified command and extraordinarily detailed planning. As soon as General Schwarz-

The Tigris River flows over a Baghdad bridge whose back has been broken by a bomb that hit dead center. In the campaign to interdict Iraqi supply lines, coalition commanders targeted fifty-four bridges; forty were destroyed and ten more damaged by precision-guided munitions.

kopf had been given overall command of coalition forces in August, he instructed the U.S. Air Force, Navy, and Marine Corps to put aside any desires to control their own air campaigns—as had been the muddled case in Vietnam. Every mission flown by every coalition plane would be a piece of a single, fully integrated plan. When Schwarzkopf named General Horner as executor of that plan he said: "We are going to have one air commander, and Horner is it."

Between August and December, a master list of about 300 targets took shape. It was based on all manner of intelligence: satellite and reconnaissance-aircraft images; reports from on-the-ground spies of the CIA and other intelligence services; the observations of Special Forces operatives who infiltrated the country; communications intercepts; consultations with academics and other visitors to Iraq; and interviews of contractors who had built bunkers, weapons-production plants, and other facilities. In many cases, the information was of blueprint exactitude: Planners knew the layouts of some key buildings and could target particular rooms with smart bombs.

Smart weaponry was critical to minimizing civilian casualties and collateral damage—a prime consideration in the planning of the campaign. But commanders were braced for some failures. Some guided bombs and missiles were bound to go astray, and unintended casualties would undoubtedly be caused by the unguided bombs that constituted the bulk of the coalition's aerial ordnance. Some intelligence failures were inevitable; the most tragic would be the destruction on February 13 of a shelter—thought to be a command bunker—that held hundreds of civilians, of whom 300 perished.

From the start of the war to its end, each day's missions were plotted out the previous evening by seventy people working at computers in the Tactical Air Control Center to generate the daily ATO. Relevant parts of the completed ATO, which ran to 700 pages on a busy day, were sent to wing commanders. Through briefings, the information percolated down to individual aircrews.

The ATO was broadly shaped by the overall priorities of the air campaign against the Iraqi infrastructure. At the outset, air-defense and C^3I targets rose to the top of the list, military-industrial targets were second in order of importance, and the interdiction of supplies third. But other factors influenced the document as well.

Weather was one. The air war had hardly begun when it was hampered by the worst storms in more than a decade. Heavy clouds moved in over southern Iraq and Kuwait and stayed there for ten days, making precision bombing difficult or impossible at times. Planes equipped with the most sophisticated bombing systems in the world were unable to spot their targets on a number of occasions and had to return home with their bombs. Sometimes visibility was so bad that planes could not even get off the ground. Hundreds of missions had to be canceled, and the air campaign fell several days behind schedule. Another factor that slowed the pace and exerted a strong influence on the ATO was the hunt for Scud launchers, made a top priority after Iraq hit Israeli cities with a flurry of the missiles on January 18. And still another shaping influence was bomb-damage assessment—determining whether a target had been destroyed or whether it needed to be hit again.

Damage information came from many sources. Often attack aircraft brought back a video record of a strike. High-flying TR-1s, descended from the 1950s-vintage U-2, and speedy RF-4, Tornado, and Mirage photoreconnaissance planes regularly overflew Iraq and took high-resolution pictures. At least five KH-11 reconnaissance satellites were maneuvered to pass over Iraq twice a day and transmit to ground stations pictures made with both visible light and infrared. From orbits up to several hundred miles above the earth, the satellites could see objects the size of golf balls. A partial antidote to the bad weather was a Lacrosse radar satellite. Although its imagery was of lower resolution than the KH-11 harvest, this satellite could see through clouds. Finally, aviators sometimes provided some low-tech evidence on their own. Early in the war, an A-7 pilot bombed a power plant, then pulled out a 35-mm camera with a zoom lens and shot photos of what he had done.

On the whole, the bomb-damage news from the field was better than good, even for the unguided "dumb bombs" that amounted to more than 90 percent of bomb tonnage delivered during the war. Usually dropped from altitudes between 8,000 and 12,000 feet, these ballistic bombs, although they sometimes went well wide of the mark, generally struck within forty feet of the target. World War II aircraft flying in the best conditions were doing well to drop their bombs within 3,300 feet of the target, on average. Smart weapons, with their laser and optical guidance, did far better. As much as 98 percent of such ordnance dropped by F-117s, for example, hit their targets, a 9,000-fold improvement over World War II results.

The Tomahawk was only slightly less reliable: Of the more than 300 fired during the course of the war—some of them from the USS

Some of the most hazardous flying in Operation Desert Wind was done by RAF Tornado GR1s against enemy airfields. Their specialty, built around an ingenious weapon system called the JP-233, involved skimming about 100 feet above a runway and ejecting two kinds of munitions from pods under the fuselage. Each pod's main punch was delivered by thirty parachute-slowed dual-charge bomblets. The first charge exploded on impact with a blast that drove the second warhead into the concrete, where it detonated to create a crater, heaves, and fractures. The second munition in each pod consisted of 215 mines that settled softly under their parachutes, righted themselves, and then detonated at preset intervals or when repair crews approached. The JP-233 was highly effective, but the low-level attack required for accuracy took the Tornadoes through such intense antiaircraft artillery fire—sometimes tens of thousands of rounds at point-blank range—that the run-

Strewn from JP-233 dispensers under a Tornado, parachute-retarded bomblets and mines float down on a target. The bomblets penetrated runway concrete to maximize their destructive effect. The mines, propping themselves upright with spring-loaded legs, presented a lingering threat amid the ruins. The warhead propelled sizable chunks of shrapnel that would disable a mine-clearing or repair vehicle such as an armored bulldozer. It also sprayed high-velocity fragments that were deadly against crews sent to undo the damage.

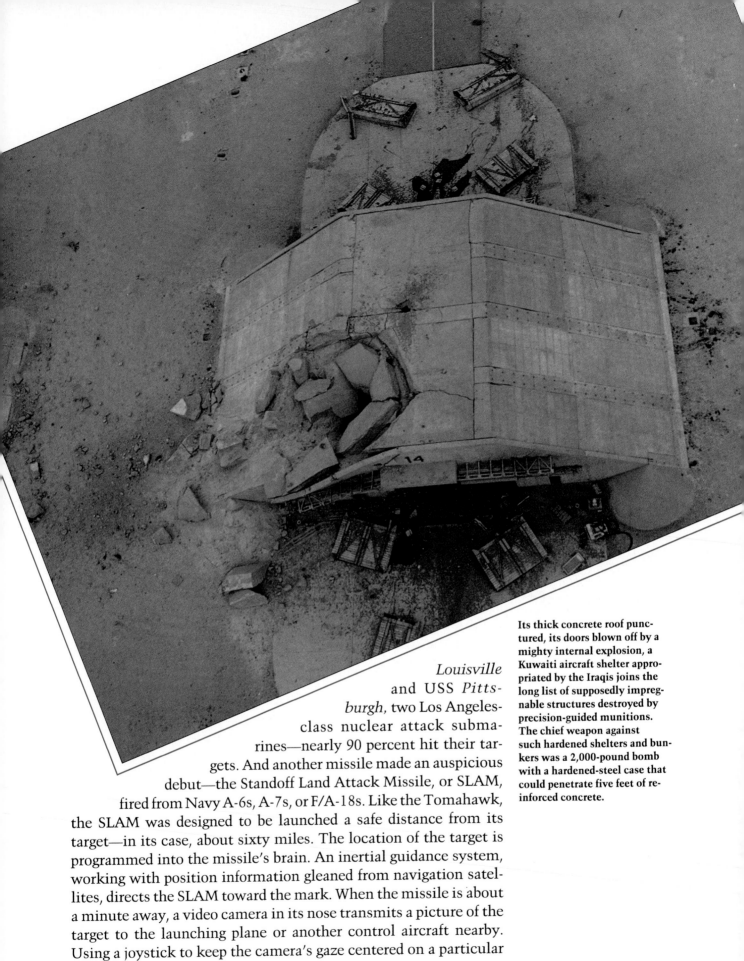

Its thick concrete roof punctured, its doors blown off by a mighty internal explosion, a Kuwaiti aircraft shelter appropriated by the Iraqis joins the long list of supposedly impregnable structures destroyed by precision-guided munitions. The chief weapon against such hardened shelters and bunkers was a 2,000-pound bomb with a hardened-steel case that could penetrate five feet of reinforced concrete.

Louisville and USS *Pittsburgh,* two Los Angeles-class nuclear attack submarines—nearly 90 percent hit their targets. And another missile made an auspicious debut—the Standoff Land Attack Missile, or SLAM, fired from Navy A-6s, A-7s, or F/A-18s. Like the Tomahawk, the SLAM was designed to be launched a safe distance from its target—in its case, about sixty miles. The location of the target is programmed into the missile's brain. An inertial guidance system, working with position information gleaned from navigation satellites, directs the SLAM toward the mark. When the missile is about a minute away, a video camera in its nose transmits a picture of the target to the launching plane or another control aircraft nearby. Using a joystick to keep the camera's gaze centered on a particular

point, the aviator controlling the missile can watch as it blasts the target with a 500-pound warhead. Furthermore, the SLAM works in cloudy weather that defeats laser-guided bombs. Flying below an overcast, the missile can find a target even if the controller cannot see the ground. The SLAM's accuracy was dramatically demonstrated during the war when two of them were directed at a hydroelectric plant. One smashed a hole in a wall; two minutes later, the second flew through the hole and exploded inside the building.

Achieving Air Supremacy

Although examples of such precision abounded, many targets had to be struck repeatedly before they were removed from the daily ATOs, and many new targets appeared on the list as the Iraqis made repairs or adjustments. General Colin Powell, chairman of the U.S. Joint Chiefs of Staff, observed, "We're dealing with an enemy that is resourceful, an enemy that knows how to work around problems, an enemy that is ingenious." New command posts were established, new communications antennas raised, new phone cable laid, damaged bridges replaced by pontoon spans. Special effort was devoted to airfields: Some badly cratered runways were put back in service within a day or so by engineers using quick-drying cement and steel reinforcements, then painted to disguise the patches.

The chief weapon against airstrips was the JP-233 cluster bomb, dropped primarily by British Tornadoes from altitudes as low as 100 feet. Inside the JP-233 are bombs in hardened-steel cases that crash through the runway before exploding to make a huge hole. These explosives are accompanied by mines designed to kill repair crews or disable bulldozers and other heavy equipment. Although Tornadoes have great speed, they were often flying into the teeth of layered SAM defenses and massed antiaircraft guns. As a result of their singularly dangerous role, they suffered a disproportionate share of losses early in the war: Four of the seventeen coalition planes downed during the first week were Tornadoes on JP-233 missions, although the British fighter-bombers accounted for less than two percent of all combat aircraft.

French Jaguars also made low-level bombing runs against airfields. On the first morning of the war, twelve Jaguars swept down on an air base in Kuwait. A SAM hit one of them in the engines,

An End to Scissors and Paste

Aircrew members have important homework to do before setting out on a bombing mission. They must chart a course that will allow them to evade enemy defenses and reach the target not only on time but with enough fuel to make it home. In the past, such planning required a stack of maps, scissors, paste, and lots of time. Laying out one sortie could take a team of two as long as fifteen hours, so numerous were the details involved. But aviators in the Persian Gulf were able to prepare strikes against Iraq and Kuwait in as little as thirty minutes.

The key to this new efficiency is the Mission Support System (MSS), a computerized planning assistant. Supplied with an up-to-date database of terrain elevations, aeronautical charts, satellite imagery, and air-defense information, the MSS uses variables keyed in by the aircrew—weapons load, altitude, and airspeed, for example—to chart the best path to and from a target. In addition, the system can show how the objective and way points along the route will appear to the pilot's own eyes or on his radar. Then the MSS prints maps and pictures of the target for the crew to study and stores the information on a cassette that is plugged into the navigation and targeting system of the aircraft before takeoff.

The MSS computer combines terrain-elevation data with satellite imagery of a target *(right)*, to show it as it will appear to a pilot on a bombing run *(below)*. In this instance, the objective is an airfield nestled against low hills as seen from 1.9 nautical miles away and 500 feet above the ground. A wedge shape on the satellite picture indicates the field of view in the low-level image; the triangle marks the target, the center of a runway. By generating a sequence of pictures from progressively closer vantage points and displaying them on a computer screen at a rate of two per second, the MSS offers the pilot a stop-action preview of his actual bombing run.

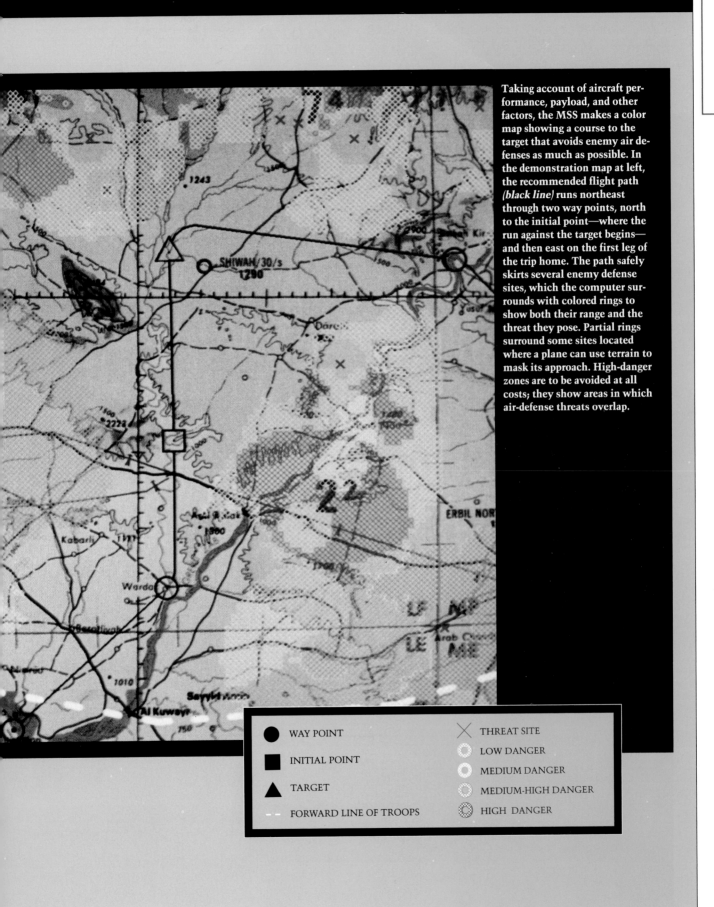

Taking account of aircraft performance, payload, and other
factors, the MSS makes a color
map showing a course to the
target that avoids enemy air defenses as much as possible. In
the demonstration map at left,
the recommended flight path
(black line) runs northeast
through two way points, north
to the initial point—where the
run against the target begins—
and then east on the first leg of
the trip home. The path safely
skirts several enemy defense
sites, which the computer sur-
rounds with colored rings to
show both their range and the
threat they pose. Partial rings
surround some sites located
where a plane can use terrain to
mask its approach. High-danger
zones are to be avoided at all
costs; they show areas in which
air-defense threats overlap.

● WAY POINT	✕ THREAT SITE
	◎ LOW DANGER
■ INITIAL POINT	◎ MEDIUM DANGER
	◎ MEDIUM-HIGH DANGER
▲ TARGET	◎ HIGH DANGER
– – FORWARD LINE OF TROOPS	

A crew chief greets his pilot after a successful mission into Iraq. During the first thirty-six hours of the war, the F-4Gs fired 268 HARM missiles at air-defense radars, destroying most of them and—as word spread among the Iraqis that radar emissions lured a killer—discouraging the use of many others. Within two weeks, coalition commanders were able to claim air supremacy—complete control of the skies.

causing a fire. An antiaircraft shell struck another in one engine. A third Jaguar took a round in the canopy; it went right through the pilot's helmet, grazing his scalp. A fourth had its flight-control system damaged. Amazingly, all four planes made it to safety.

Iraqi planes rarely came up to challenge the attackers, and when they did, the outcome was lopsided. In the first seven days of the conflict, coalition fighters knocked down sixteen enemy planes without a single loss in air-to-air combat. Not only was Saddam's Air Force inferior at this demanding martial art, but the dictator showed little inclination to mount an aerial defense—in part because he was sure that the cream of his Air Force would be safe on the ground, invulnerable in about 300 shelters that had been built by Dutch, British, and Yugoslavian construction firms. Buried under great piles of sand, the fortified hangars shielded planes under steel-and-concrete roofs ranging in thickness from four to twelve feet. The steel doors were two feet thick and weighed forty tons. Protecting the doors were concrete blast walls two feet thick.

A pivotal moment in the suppression of the Iraqi Air Force came nine days into the conflict, when coalition planes began bombing the shelters with laser-guided 2,000-pound bombs built with hardened-steel cases that allowed them to penetrate the roofs before being detonated by delayed-action fuzes. The bombs were spectacularly effective. Iraqi planes began fleeing to Iran. Many escaped before coalition fighters could intercept them. Over twenty-four days, 122 planes would make it out of the country, only to be impounded by the Iranians. (After the war, Iran would keep most of them, overpainting the Iraqi insignia.) Not every fugitive arrived safely; nineteen would be shot down before reaching sanctuary.

The Iraqi Air Force was finished. From now on, the coalition forces could bomb almost at will. And bomb they did, tearing apart the military apparatus on which Saddam Hussein had spent $50 billion and bludgeoning the supporting industries. Fighter-bombers flattened barracks, arms factories, chemical plants, refineries. Day after day, they ripped into the military-industrial complex in the suburbs of Baghdad and an industrial archipelago between the cities of Mosul, Kirkuk, and Tikrit. Night after night, the F-117s—Ghost Riders and Night Stalkers, the two squadrons called themselves— slipped into enemy air space to deliver their pinpoint blows.

Nuclear facilities in Iraq—strongly defended from the outset, given Israel's 1981 destruction of the Osirak reactor—were slated for a devastating pounding. SAM and AAA fire made the job a tough one. Around such high-value targets, the Iraqis conscientiously repaired or replaced damaged fire-control radars, making the ground-fire more accurate than that encountered near less important objectives. Eight flights of four F-16s, each armed with unguided bombs, had a go one day at a cluster of four nuclear reactors south of Baghdad. Smoke pots obscured the target, and antiaircraft fire was intense, so the fighter-bombers turned back. In short order, the same mission fell to eight stealth fighters, which sneaked in the following night, when the smoke pots were idle, to wreck three of the reactors. The fourth succumbed to a later F-117 raid.

About the tenth day of the war, the emphasis of the daily ATO began shifting to the interdiction of supplies to the Iraqi forces in southern Iraq and Kuwait. Coalition planes cut roads and railway lines, smashed bridges across the rivers, and blasted fuel depots and ammunition dumps. One such cache erupted with such violence that the flash was seen 200 miles away in Saudi Arabia.

On January 30, General Schwarzkopf summed up the results of fourteen days of the air war—more than 30,000 sorties in all. "The Iraqi early warning system has completely failed," he said. The only aircraft taking off were those attempting to escape to Iran. Military communications were so degraded that corps commanders were often unable to speak to their divisional subordinates. Sixty percent of "leadership targets"—headquarters, intelligence centers, and the like—had been severely damaged or destroyed. A quarter of Iraq's power plants were out of action, and another quarter had been "adversely affected." All of Iraq's nuclear facilities were demolished, as were more than half of the facilities for chemical and biological weapons. The flow of supplies to troops in Kuwait had been cut to 2,000 tons per day, one-tenth the volume needed.

A week after the inauguration of the air campaign, General Colin Powell had summed up coalition strategy in blunt and vivid language: "First we're going to cut it off, and then we're going to kill it." The full realization of that strategy would require another month of warfare in the air and, ultimately, on the ground. But after just two weeks of air strikes—an aerial campaign such as the world had never seen before—the command-and-control structure of Saddam Hussein's enormous military lay in ruins. ★

Alone into the Lion's Den

In an age of missiles and laser-guided bombs carried by aircraft packed with electronic aids for the crew, the task of destroying targets on the ground remains difficult and dangerous. Smart weapons—which can often be loosed far from a target and outside the enemy's most intensive air defenses—are not suitable for use on every sort of target. Railroad yards, warehouses, and petroleum storage facilities, for example, are best attacked with relatively simple weapons that require aircrews to drop them right down the enemy's throat, straight into the teeth of radar-directed antiaircraft defenses, a feat that demands skill, determination, and daring.

One of the most demanding types of mission, illustrated on the following pages, is the solo "hi-lo-lo-hi" night attack. On such an assignment, a fighter-bomber enters enemy air space at a fuel-conserving 25,000 feet or so and descends to a height as little as 200 feet above the ground to elude enemy radar while approaching the initial point (IP), the starting point for the actual attack. Popping up to an altitude of several thousand feet, the jet makes a diving attack, then streaks away at low level until safely out of range of enemy air defenses. For the rest of the flight home, the pilot climbs again to higher altitude to save fuel.

Arguably the best plane for such missions is the two-seat F-15E Strike Eagle. An all-weather fighter-bomber derived from the single-seat F-15C air-superiority fighter, the F-15E uses an inertial navigation system (INS) and LANTIRN *(pages 64-65)* for flying and bombing at night. It also has terrain-following radar for low-level flight to elude enemy radar. With this equipment as well as electronic gear to detect and jam enemy radar, the F-15E can penetrate enemy defenses unescorted. Flown by a seasoned crew, the plane and its computerized bombing system can deliver even unguided weapons with extraordinary precision—typically within thirty feet or so of the aim point.

Down into the Weeds

Nearing enemy air defenses, the pilot of an F-15E descends from a fuel-efficient cruising altitude of 25,000 feet. His intention is to fly below a ridgeline, making it difficult for enemy air defenses guarding the approach to the target to get off a good shot.

As the plane passes through 2,000 feet, the pilot activates the terrain-following radar in the LANTIRN navigation pod. To help conceal the F-15 from the searching eyes of enemy radar, this system keeps the plane at a fixed height above the ground while the pilot, guided by the FLIR image from the LANTIRN navigation pod, steers his course. For this mission, he has selected the lowest height the terrain-following system permits: 200 feet.

On the way to this altitude, however, an alarm generated by the tactical electronic warfare system (TEWS) tells the pilot and weapons systems officer (WSO) flying in the backseat of the F-15 that they have been detected by a search radar. The plane is safely behind the ridge before a SAM site linked to the search radar can fire a missile, but seconds later, as the fighter-bomber speeds across a gap in the ridge at nearly 500 knots, the SAM battery locks on. In the cockpit, the TEWS sounds another tone, warning of a missile launch. As planned, the aircraft again passes behind the ridge, and with no target in view, the missile explodes well above and behind the F-15. A second missile, fired through another gap in the ridgeline, also misses.

Breaking for the Target

Approaching the IP—a road intersection four miles from the target—the F-15 continues to elude enemy radar as it snakes along 800 feet below the top of a cliff. In the backseat, the WSO monitors a miles-to-go readout on the INS that counts down the distance to the IP. The pilot, meanwhile, arms the bombing system and watches for the crossroad to appear in the FLIR display on the HUD.

As the jet streaks across the IP, the pilot pulls the plane into a steep climb. At the same time, the WSO switches the LANTIRN system from the navigation pod to the targeting pod so the instrument can lock its gaze onto the target—a complex of fuel-storage tanks.

Banking toward the tank farm, the F-15 appears on the screens of air-defense radars directing rapid-firing four-barrel 23-mm and longer-range 57-mm antiaircraft guns arrayed in defense of the target. Warning tones shriek in the crew's headphones, and almost immediately flak begins to blossom in the night sky dangerously close to the now-vulnerable plane.

111

The Objective in Sight

To avoid the bursting flak, the Eagle jinks sharply every few seconds to throw off the guns trying to track it. Despite the brutal maneuvering, the crew must nevertheless locate and confirm the target by monitoring LANTIRN displays.

At a height of 12,000 feet above the plateau, the highest point of the F-15's climb, the pilot noses the aircraft over into a dive toward the fuel dump. Doing so gives the LANTIRN targeting pod an unobstructed view of the target.

The LANTIRN system uses target coordinates, programmed into the F-15's INS equipment before the mission, to point the targeting pod's FLIR sensor at the fuel dump. Locking onto the target, the system draws a box around the image of the tank farm as it appears on the HUD *(inset).* As the pilot maneuvers the aircraft toward this target box, he rechecks that the bombing system is armed, then he and the WSO check the FLIR image to confirm that the LANTIRN system has correctly identified the focus of the attack.

The view out the front. As the pilot banks toward the tank farm in the target box, the HUD displays information critical to flying the plane and hitting the mark. For a bull's-eye, the pilot must steer so that the vertical line in the center of the HUD passes through the tank farm. The lower end of the line is the pipper. It lies at the center of a circle divided into 1,000-foot increments of slant range—the distance from the aircraft to the target. The letters CDIP (continuously displayed impact point) mean that the pipper shows the pilot where his bombs would strike if released. A cross below a horizontal line showing heading (ten degrees) confirms that the system is armed. Canted lines indicate the angle of bank and—along with a small circle called the velocity vector (atop the vertical line)—the dive angle. Down the left side of the HUD appear airspeed (480 knots), mach number (.830), present G-loading (1.0), and maximum loading permitted considering the weapons aboard (9.0). Altitude—12,000 feet—appears in the upper right corner.

Lining Up
for the Drop

Now descending through 10,000 feet at 480 knots, the Eagle has stabilized its dive angle at forty-five degrees. The vertical line on the HUD transfixes the tank farm, but the pilot cannot yet drop his bombs. Slowed by drag and accelerated earthward by gravity immediately upon release, the weapons would fall short of the target, as shown by the position of the pipper. In order to advance the pipper to the target, the pilot must fly a straight course, making this part of the mission the most hazardous. During these four or five seconds, the defenders have their best chance to score against the attacking plane, which cannot take evasive action without spoiling its aim. As the range decreases, the pipper—pilots call it the "death dot"—advances on the target.

Bombs Away

When the pipper coincides with the target, the pilot presses the pickle button on the control stick and holds it down. The automatic bombing system then takes over and, after about a half second of "settling time," releases the bombs. To spread ordnance across the target, the aircrew programmed the automatic bombing system before takeoff to release four of the bombs, pause for one second, then drop the others.

As the pilot presses the pickle button, the target box vanishes from the HUD and two new symbols appear. One, a diamond, marks the spot where the opening salvo of bombs will strike the ground; the second group will impact a couple of hundred yards farther into the tank farm.

The other new symbol—a horizontal mark on the vertical line—is called the frag cue. The pilot must keep the velocity vector above this mark or risk falling victim to debris from his own exploding ordnance. As the F-15 continues its dive between salvos, the frag cue moves nearer the velocity vector. So, when the pilot feels the last bombs lurch free, he hauls back on the stick to pull out of his dive—and then breaks to the left.

When the bombs explode,
approximately fifteen seconds
after the pilot pickled them off,
the F-15E Strike Eagle is already
two miles into the flight back
to its home base.

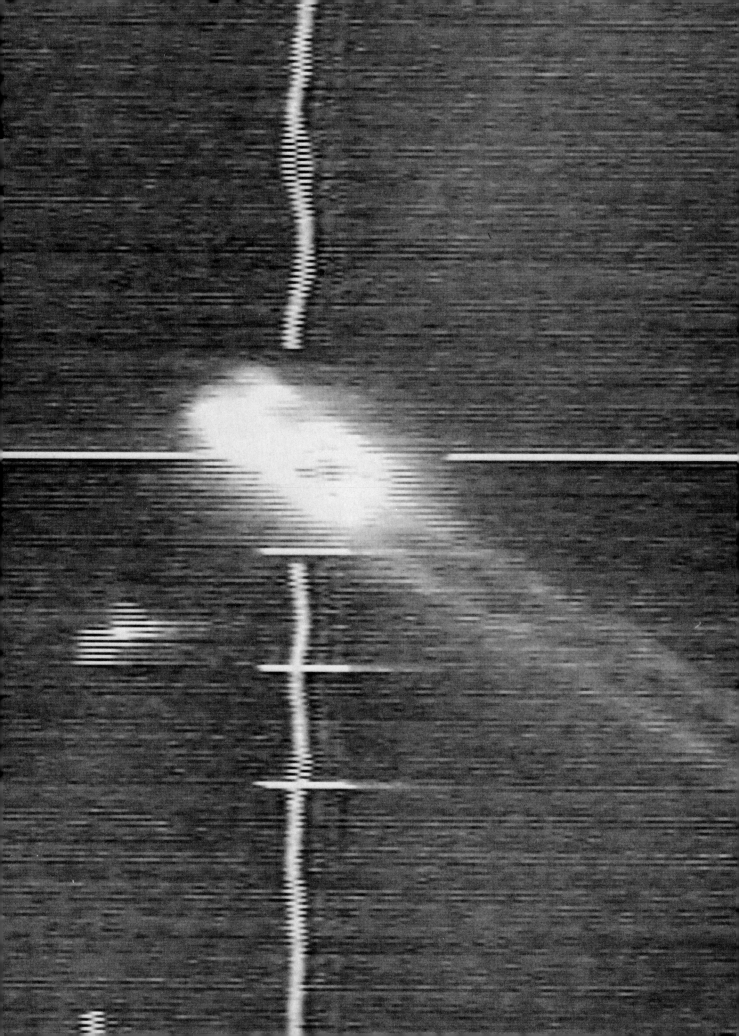

Modern Air Power Triumphant

Milliseconds from oblivion, a speeding Iraqi tracked vehicle glows hot in a view from the infrared seeker of a Maverick missile carried by the F-16 fighter-bomber that, seconds earlier, launched the Maverick that is about to strike. The sensitivity of the missile's infrared imaging system can be seen from streaks trailing behind the vehicle, the result of its tracks churning the cool desert surface to uncover sand still warm from the daytime sun.

Armed with four 1,000-pound bombs destined for a heavily defended position in Iraq just north of Kuwait, the Saudi GR1 Tornado barreled along at low level. The two-man crew expected the enemy to be alert, and they were not disappointed. When the Tornado was still several miles from the target, the ground suddenly came alive with the deadly twinkle of hundreds upon hundreds of antiaircraft weapons, fired blindly in the hope of catching some luckless attacker in a barrage of projectiles. But against the moon and some miles to the north, the Tornado crew could see the signature of other allied raiders that night—contrails of three fast-moving U.S. Air Force B-52s sent to carpet-bomb the area. From the meticulous choreography of the day's Air Tasking Order, the Tornado crew, young officers in combat for the first time, knew what was coming.

In the blink of an eye, the earth seemed to burst open its molten core. A typical load for a three-ship cell of B-52s consisted of 153 bombs, fifty-one to a plane. Most of them were 500-pound, general-purpose Mk 82s, each detonating with a brilliant flash that gouged a twenty-five-foot-wide crater in the desert and sprayed white-hot shrapnel 3,000 feet in every direction. Interspersed among the Mk 82 bursts sparkled hundreds upon hundreds of antiarmor and antipersonnel bomblets strewn from CBU-87 cluster-bomb canisters. The whole load could be released within a few seconds, typically saturating a box 1,000 feet by 6,000 feet. Moments later, as the Saudi Tornado arrowed in to lay its ordnance on the target, not a single antiaircraft weapon remained firing. "They all stopped," reported the Saudi pilot, and noted that he and his backseater could see a similar B-52 strike going in seventy miles away.

There is no testimony from the unfortunate Iraqis upon whose heads doom descended that night early in Operation Desert Wind, but in Vietnam, some survivors of the hammering overpressures were captured as they meandered aimlessly, dazed and bleeding at the nose and mouth. Among soldiers who considered themselves at risk of such abuse, morale crumbled like a sandcastle in the surf.

After obliterating Iraq's military infrastructure and degrading its Air Force and antiaircraft defenses, the next order of business for air power in the Gulf War was to shatter the morale and demolish the equipment of the world's fourth-largest army. Most particularly, the target would be Saddam Hussein's vaunted 150,000-man Republican Guard, fanatically loyal veterans of the Iranian war, well trained and equipped with the best Soviet tanks Saddam could buy. Some experts rated the Republican Guard superior to—or at least the equal of—topline U.S. and Soviet armored divisions.

The air assault against the Iraqi Army would begin on the first day of the war and would proceed in stages from north to south. "The idea," as Lieutenant General Charles Horner grimly put it, "is to feed the enemy in bite-sized chunks for the ground forces to devour." Air power would chop up the mobile reserves positioned in southern Iraq and central Kuwait; the planes would then prepare the battleground itself by striking at the entrenched enemy along the Kuwaiti border with Saudi Arabia; and finally, when the land war began, the United States and its coalition partners would bring overwhelming air power to bear to support their advancing troops.

Desert Wind would not be so neatly compartmented, of course. War never is. In the swirling, all-out aerial onslaught, priorities would shift and many things would happen simultaneously: Certain enemy positions in Kuwait would be hit while the bombers were still pounding the Republican Guard reserve in Iraq; and close air support missions would help defeat an ill-considered Iraqi thrust across the Saudi border almost a month before the ground war started. Commanders and aircrews would exhibit surprising flexibility and resourcefulness in evolving fresh tactics.

Many aircraft would be pressed into new roles that might surprise their designers. The mach 2.5 swing-wing F-111 Aardvark, intended for deep strikes into Eastern Europe, would be armed with laser-guided Paveway bombs to become a "tank-plinker" nonpareil. The swift, nimble F-16 Falcon fighter-bomber would win new laurels as a forward air controller, a "fast FAC" patrolling "kill boxes" to pinpoint the elusive enemy. And the glamourless A-10 Warthog, the unsophisticated "red-headed stepchild of the Air Force," as someone once called it, would emerge as a hero of the action, not only fulfilling its role as a cannon-packing daytime tank buster but successfully stalking the enemy at night in an unexpected way—through the eyes of Maverick missiles.

Nourishing the swarms of "shooters," in Air Force parlance, would be the greatest aerial refueling operation in history. And orchestrating all the action would be not only the omnipresent, all-seeing AWACS but also a prototype airborne surveillance system called JSTARS, for Joint Surveillance and Target Attack Radar System. The nucleus of JSTARS, which existed only as two unproven prototypes, was a special radar capable of detecting trucks and tanks at distances up to 200 miles, whether they were on the move or playing possum *(pages 148-149)*. Installed in a military version of the Boeing 707 airliner, the two JSTARS planes, designated E-8As, were rushed to Saudi Arabia before testing stateside was even half-completed.

The Destruction Begins

JSTARS proved its worth from day one, pinpointing massive enemy formations for the first strike packages to hit the Iraqi Army. Thundering aloft from Saudi Arabian bases at 2:00 a.m. on January 17, they rendezvoused with their tankers in darkness and were over the targets in Iraq and Kuwait at dawn. Aircrews had been briefed on what to expect, but they were not fully prepared for the scene that greeted them. As far as the eye could see, the desert was aswarm with tanks, armored personnel carriers, trucks, and other equipment, some of it in revetments or under camouflage netting, but the bulk clustered around unit headquarters and supply dumps. "Definitely a target-rich environment," said one Falcon pilot.

Each strike package was a self-contained micro-air force of two dozen or more F-16s supported and defended by a mix of F-15C Eagle escorts, EF-111 Raven electronic jammers, and F-4G Wild Weasel radar-suppression craft. Ten minutes after one strike formation crossed into Iraq, an orbiting AWACS flashed a warning that two MiG-29 Fulcrums were on an attack heading. The Fulcrums were top-of-the-line Soviet-supplied fighters, the newest and most capable aircraft in the Iraqi inventory, but they were swiftly eliminated by AIM-7 radar-guided Sparrow missiles launched from F-15s sweeping ahead of the strike force. Another two MiG-29s came to grief when one Iraqi pilot mistakenly shot down his wingman while attempting to zero in on some approaching raiders and then inexplicably followed the first plane to a fiery death.

With no further interference from fighters, the formations raced on to their goals, with the EF-111s filling enemy radar screens with a snowstorm of static. As the F-16s rolled in on their objectives from about 12,000 feet, the F-4G Wild Weasels above them launched high-speed antiradiation missiles to destroy the radar stations themselves. Then the ground erupted with tremendous explosions in all target areas, as the fighter-bombers swept back up through a sky rapidly filling with SAMs and the puffy white airbursts of antiaircraft artillery that pilots likened to popcorn. With or without radar to aim their weapons, the Iraqis were cutting loose with everything they had—and it amounted to an astounding volume of fire. Pilots of one squadron estimated that eighty SAMs were fired at them during their mission. None hit, but one missile came close enough to an F-16 for the pilot to notice the green-painted fins as the thing whipped past. A colonel leading an F-16 squadron acknowledged that it was "one of the five scariest missions I've ever flown." Miraculously, none of the planes were hit.

Flak or no, initial appraisals of bomb damage told of enormous destruction. Pilots reported turning hundreds of tanks and other vehicles into charred hulks. Strike-assessment videotape confirmed that and more: scores of twisted artillery pieces, ravaged supply convoys, shattered headquarters bunkers, exploding ammunition that filled the sky with fireworks, and burning fuel dumps that sent greasy black smoke 20,000 feet into the air.

But then, as plans were laid for the second day of the air assault, the weather turned sour. During the fourteen years that the U.S. Air Force had been monitoring meteorological conditions in the Persian Gulf, January and February had been cool and dry. Yet on January 18, an unusual confluence of air masses brought thick, low clouds and heavy rains to the Middle East. Storms continued sporadically for ten days. On the first day of poor weather, for example, a strike of more than forty Marine F/A-18 Hornets returned to its Saudi base without dropping its ordnance.

The respite afforded Iraqis was by no means total. Numerous breaks in the overcast permitted shooters to descend on enemy armored formations, although pilots who found targets often had difficulty judging the extent of the damage they caused. Under such conditions, dumb bombs were more useful than smart weapons.

Getting a rousing send-off, an F-16 pilot taxis past his whooping, cheering ground crew on the way to pound the Iraqi Army a few days before the beginning of the ground war. Fitted with a LANTIRN navigation pod, the aircraft carries a tank-busting Maverick missile and a fuel tank under each of its wings. Two wing-tip-mounted Sidewinder air-to-air missiles go along in case of an encounter with Iraqi jets.

Laser designators and infrared sensors alike could not penetrate the clouds, and ranging below the overcast to search out targets for laser-guided Paveways and infrared-homing Maverick missiles would overexpose aircraft to deadly sheets of flak. Of course, none of these hindrances affected the three- and six-plane formations of B-52s operating from Morón, Spain, from Diego Garcia in the Indian Ocean, and from a Royal Air Force base at Fairford, England. Altogether, forty-eight of the intercontinental bombers would be sent to war, and any of them could find its own way to a bomb-release point, regardless of the weather, or be guided there by radar.

Overall, however, the unexpectedly poor flying conditions upset the timetable for reducing the Iraqi Army. Coalition planners had counted on a mounting crescendo of between 2,500 and 3,000 sorties daily, of which 300 to 350 were to be directed at the Republican Guard and other units. Yet between January 18 and 28, the actual strikes flown were limited to an average of fewer than 1,900 daily.

A Challenging Game of Cat and Mouse

Meanwhile, Saddam Hussein was playing his wild card—and it was one that would further impede air power in its mission to diminish the Iraqi Army. The war was only hours old when long-range Iraqi al-Hussein and al-Abbas ballistic missiles began arcing toward Saudi Arabia and Israel from fixed pads and mobile launchers. The weapons were modifications of Soviet-built Scud missiles and usually went by the same name. Descended from Germany's V-2 rocket of World War II, the liquid-fuel Scud and its Iraqi derivatives were highly inaccurate; after a flight of 500 miles, such a missile stood about a fifty-fifty chance of striking within a mile and a half of the target. Moreover, they proved vulnerable to the U.S. Patriot anti-missile system. Nevertheless, with the potential to carry chemical warheads, Saddam's long-range missiles could sow terror throughout Saudi and Israeli population centers. If something was not done to deal quickly with the menace, Israel threatened to intervene, a course that could drive more than one Arab state from the coalition arrayed against Iraq. The United States was determined that Israel stay out of the war, and thus began the Great Scud Chase.

Prewar intelligence estimates suggested that there were perhaps 100 Scuds in Iraq's inventory, and it was no secret that the weapons had to be fired from certain "launch boxes" in northwestern and southeastern Iraq in order to reach targets in Israel and Saudi Arabia. All the fixed pads and reloadable transporter/erector/launchers (TELs) that could be identified were pulverized during the opening hours of the campaign, but the continuing volume of launches—as many as ten in one night—made it apparent that Iraq had many more missiles and TELs than anyone guessed. Moreover, the launchers were hard to find. During the day, the mobile TELs would be hidden under bridges or in culverts and buildings. Others were disguised to resemble tank-trucks, semitrailers, concrete carriers, even railroad cars. At night, they would be moved into position, and the missiles would be fueled and launched.

"Finding them," said one pilot, "was like hunting for needles in a haystack." By day, flights of A-10 Warthogs rumbled up and down roads crossing the launch box, blasting anything that might conceal a launcher. Every once in a while they hit pay dirt. On the second day of the war, a pair of A-10s ducked under the weather to surprise three mobile launchers parked in the open by a road, the crews no doubt thinking the overcast would conceal them. Each pilot made four or five passes at the launchers, chewing them up with 30-mm cannon fire, Mavericks, and cluster bombs. With time spent avoiding groundfire, the operation took about half an hour. Another seven Scuds were destroyed by A-10s during the first week.

By night, pairs of F-15E Strike Eagles teamed up with the E-8A JSTARS radar-surveillance planes to patrol the launch boxes. Some nights, as many as twenty-four of the fighter-bombers would be on Scud-hunting missions, orbiting in racetrack patterns, taking regular sips of fuel from a tanker and awaiting word from JSTARS. On some nights, the F-15s waited in vain for a vector toward a Scud site, but usually there was plenty of business.

When the Iraqis brought their missiles out of hiding, the F-15s

At a Saudi air base, munitions specialists install nose fuzes and arming wires on a pair of 500-pound Mk 82 iron, or unguided, bombs before loading them on a trailer for transport to the aircraft. Ordinarily, fuzes were set for a quarter-second delay to ensure target penetration before triggering the bomb's 200-pound high-explosive charge.

pounced. The weapon of choice was the 2,000-pound Paveway laser-guided bomb. It was especially effective against missiles that were all but ready to launch. "Even a near miss with all that volatile fuel aboard was close enough," said one pilot. "There would be a huge secondary explosion. You could see it miles away."

Sometimes, a Strike Eagle crew sent to attack a Scud launcher detected by JSTARS arrived just as the missile was launched. On one memorable occasion, an F-15 pilot thought a Scud was a SAM fired at him. Wrenching his plane into a hard break, he snapped on his jamming system. Only when the exhaust glow continued long after a SAM would have spent its fuel did he realize that the missile was a Scud and radioed AWACS. Already, however, other Eagles on Scud watch were flashing toward the launcher to take it out.

In the event that the Iraqis managed to fire a Scud before JSTARS could pinpoint the launcher, the heat from the missile's exhaust tripped infrared sensors of the Defense Support Program Satellite System, in constant attendance 22,300 miles up in space. The satellite whose field of view encompassed Iraq tracked the Scud and sent the data to a ground station in Colorado, where computers calculated the launch point. The information was quickly transmitted to an AWACS in the combat zone, which dispatched the F-15s—often within sixty seconds of the launch. The pilot had only to punch the launch-site coordinates into his navigation system, and the plane showed him the direction and distance to the target.

Aircrews brought home videotapes of the targets growing larger in the image produced by the LANTIRN targeting pods (pages 64-65). One WSO in the backseat called out, "That's a Mr. TEL, all right. Fire the pickle whenever"; the pilot responded, "Looking good. Mr. Scud is on the TEL." Then came the lurching, side-to-side "clunk-clunk" as the bombs left the racks. On the screen, an explosion of fire and debris engulfed the target.

On one occasion, in particularly bad weather, a three-ship cell of B-52s was diverted from another mission to radar-bomb launch sites with their thirty-ton payloads. At a Pentagon briefing, a newsman asked Lieutenant General Thomas Kelly, operations director for the Joint Chiefs of Staff, if this was not a little like using a sledgehammer to swat a fly. Kelly's reply: "My own personal opinion is that's a delightful way to kill a fly."

The sledgehammering of the flies proceeded to the very end of the war, and while the B-52s, Eagles, and Warthogs never totally wiped out the Scuds, they reduced the number of launches from an average of five per night in the beginning to barely one per night. Yet the Great Scud Chase, for all its political importance, was a military sideshow. In the main arena, the B-52s and the fighter-bombers were systematically destroying Saddam Hussein's Republican Guard and the rest of his army as well.

A Change in the Weather

By the last week in January, skies had cleared sufficiently for coalition air forces to begin stepping up the air campaign. The B-52 effort was formidable. Beginning at sunset, the huge bombers appeared overhead every few hours. Saudi soldiers posted near the Kuwaiti border gleefully awaited the nightly raids, calling them the "six o'clock boom." On January 29, twenty-one B-52s dropped 315 tons of bombs; the next night, twenty-eight sorties pickled off 470 tons. And to usher in February, six waves of B-52s unloaded no less than 500 tons of destruction on the Republican Guard and its supply dumps. Reporting the secondary explosion caused by seventeen 1,000-pound bombs impacting a site, an Air Force liaison officer near the Kuwaiti border said that he could see the fireball from forty miles away. Another observer noted a flash that turned out to be an ammo dump going up 200 miles distant; it was later rated as one of the biggest nonnuclear explosions in history.

In the view of some officers, the B-52s were "the safest, most effective way to go after the Republican Guard." But while the big bombers were deadly against masses of armor in the open, nothing but a direct hit could ensure the destruction of tanks and other weapons surrounded by berms up to twelve feet high. And so the fighter-bombers continued to go in by the score to hammer the enemy day and night with their precision delivery systems—everything meticulously integrated by the daily ATO.

Pilots flying by day described a terrible scene: clusters of burned-out tanks, wrecked artillery batteries, fuel depots and munitions dumps shrouded in smoke. "It's just a big, long swath of craters," said an F-16 squadron commander. "There's a bunch of them out there. They extend from the border as far north as you can go."

There was no letup. In Riyadh, millions upon millions of bits of information were fed into the computer banks at General Horner's headquarters. AWACS planes—a dozen or so were assigned to the air war—provided airborne command and control twenty-four hours a day; nothing aloft escaped their unblinking eyes. The two E-8A JSTARS aircraft were aloft twenty hours of each day, scanning 600,000 square miles every twelve hours; anything that moved on the ground—and much that did not—showed up on the consoles. All this, plus satellite intelligence, pilot reports, and information from a dozen other sources, was funneled to shifts of seventy planning experts. They assigned targets and scheduled strikes and aerial refuelings. In Vietnam, by the time a target list returned from Washington approved for action, mission planning sometimes took days. The massive use of computers on the scene in Desert Wind made it possible to lay on complex missions in a few hours.

So intense was the effort and so superbly was it coordinated that one F-16 flight leader reported an occasion when four of his planes were working west to east across a target while four other F-16s were going north to south across a separate target just a short distance away. "I looked over and saw bombs impacting off to the side and thought my guys had messed up," the pilot said. "But the bombs were from someone else working nearby." In the dense traffic, every flier worried about ramming another plane. But to its everlasting credit, AWACS kept everything unscrambled, and while there were a number of near misses—including one in which an F-15 zipped within 500 feet of an AWACS—there would not be a single midair collision during the entire forty-three-day war.

All systems, in fact, were performing far beyond expectations. Virtually every aircraft type showed a readiness rate of 85 percent or better, at least 10 percent higher than can be maintained economically in peacetime. Much of the credit for this performance goes to tireless ground crews and supply people. On every flight line, in every hangar and repair shop, they worked flat-out to keep the aircraft flying. The Military Airlift Command's pipeline for spare parts was nothing short of phenomenal; MAC's "Desert Express" could whisk a part from a stateside supply depot to a mechanic's repair stand in Saudi Arabia within forty-eight hours.

Superb maintenance aside, the aircraft themselves were operating with astonishing durability and effectiveness. The 250 F-16 Falcons deployed to Saudi Arabia proved so reliable that one pilot reported an amazing twenty-eight sorties in twenty-seven days without so much as a late takeoff. The Falcon had long since received its baptism of fire with the Israeli Air Force in the conflicts of the 1980s, so its strengths were well known. But other aircraft that had never undergone the test of battle were quickly validating their design concepts and hardware. The Navy's F/A-18 Hornet, designed for double duty as fighter and attack platform, neatly certified itself on one strike mission when a pilot was warned of an oncoming MiG-23 Flogger. Turning dogfighter, the Hornet pilot coolly shot down the MiG with a Sparrow missile, then switched to the attack mode and howled down to deliver his ordnance.

But the pilots with the biggest grins were the drivers of the old A-10 Warthog, 132 of which were hurled into the air war. Lacking radar or other advanced internal sensors, the twenty-year-old design had been built for only one mission—to destroy tanks in daylight at low level on the plains of Europe. Pilots of sleek, supersonic fighters hooted at its lumbering, 400-knot top speed and ungainly, stub-winged appearance. But not the men who flew it. One major who transferred from F-4 Phantoms said that he had increasingly felt like a chauffeur taking his weapons systems officer to work. "All the neat toys were in the WSO's cockpit, and all I did was drive the jet around while he did all the fun stuff." But with the A-10, the major continued, "It's just me and the jet, and there's very, very, very few electrons moving around, no autopilot, no magic, no radars, no cosmic stuff. If something blows up, it's because I hit it."

In their combat debut, the Warthogs and pilots danced through the flak to scourge enemy formations. The potent 30-mm cannons, firing two-pound depleted-uranium slugs, punched effortlessly through the top and side armor of Iraqi tanks. Normal practice was to trigger the gun in a thirty- to forty-degree dive in a "high-angle strafe" after approaching within 3,000 feet of the target. At that range the gun was uniformly lethal, and some pilots were killing tanks as far away as 9,000 feet.

One A-10 jockey became an instant celebrity by knocking down an Iraqi helicopter with his gun. On the first pass, the pilot tried to hit the chopper with an AIM-9 Sidewinder, carried to give the Warthog a measure of self-defense if challenged by an enemy fighter. But the missile's heat seeker failed to lock on. Coming around again, the pilot armed his cannon. "Some of the bullets went through him, but I couldn't be sure," said the pilot. "So I came back with the final pass, hit it, and it fell apart." He could not identify the helicopter, he confessed, because "it was just a bunch of little pieces."

A pair of deadly Rockeye cluster bombs, each of which is capable of dispensing 247 armor-piercing bomblets over an area of 5,000 square yards, nestles under the wing of an F-15E Strike Eagle. The specialist at right is tightening a sway brace that keeps the bomb rigid on the pylon; the protective green shroud at far right covers the lens of a LANTIRN pod that enables the crew to find and hit targets in total darkness.

Complementing the A-10's cannon was a second antitank weapon—the AGM-65 Maverick air-to-ground missile. Early versions were TV-guided and thus restricted to daylight operations. But in the late 1980s, an imaging infrared guidance system had been fitted to the Maverick in the thought of making it more effective in haze or fog and against camouflaged targets that the pilot first saw with his own eyes.

For the next few years, the new IR Maverick continued to be a daytime weapon. But shortly after deploying to Saudi Arabia for possible action against masses of Iraqi armor protected by a formidable air defense, Warthog pilots tried using the infrared-sensitive eye of the Maverick to hunt tanks at night, when antiaircraft fire would be less effective.

Doubts about the idea centered on the missile's seeker. Intended to be pointed at a target by the pilot rather than to help him find targets as the LANTIRN system does, the seeker could be aimed in different directions only by maneuvering the aircraft. Furthermore, surveying the landscape through the narrow, 2.5-degree field of view afforded by the seeker optics was, said one practitioner of the art, "a little like looking through a soda straw." Yet a technique evolved in which the Warthog pilot put his plane into a shallow dive and then began to "root around," sweeping the seeker across the terrain below by banking the plane first one way, then the other.

Though crude, the routine worked. When war came, the A-10s—as well as some F-16s, which had also been conceived as day fighters—joined the FLIR-equipped F-111s and F-15Es in devastating, round-the-clock attacks on the Iraqi Army. Operating with JSTARS, flights of A-10s would enter a target-filled sector at 10,000 feet or so, then switch on the Maverick. Thereafter, the procedure varied with the pilot. One Warthog driver called his approach the altitude-and-ten formula. "For example," he explained, "if I'm at 6,000 feet, then at six miles I'll push over ten degrees. Putting the nose that low below the horizon will keep the missile in the target area and then I start looking." A search took time, but when the seeker found something, the pilot would put his cross hairs on the target, bore in, and fire off the Maverick.

The technique was strictly ad lib, but it killed hundreds of

tanks. The Air Force reported that the sleek white Mavericks were achieving "catastrophic kills" 80 per- cent of the time. No tank could with- stand the missile's 125-pound shaped- charge warhead. And there were variations on the theme. Having expended their Mav- ericks, pilots often lit up the area with parachute flares. That made it possible to go visual and hit other targets with their cannons, 500-pound iron bombs, and Rockeye antiarmor cluster bombs.

With baleful visage, an A-10 Thunderbolt II fighter-bomber joins the hunt for tanks during the Gulf War. Better known as Warthogs for their unlovely lines, the 150 A-10s committed to the fight emerged as the top killers of Iraqi armor, credited with 1,000 tanks, or 58 percent of those destroyed from the air. The pod suspended below the cockpit of the A-10 above is a laser detector used by the pilot to find a target being illuminat- ed by a laser in another aircraft or on the ground.

How effective the A-10s could be at night was amply demon- strated late in January, during the ill-starred Iraqi attack on the Saudi border town of Khafji. A flight of A-10s was sent in to hit a column of twenty-four enemy tanks attempting to join the battle. After the first runs, the pilots no longer needed their Mavericks to see the enemy. The fires were so bright that everything down below was clearly visible. The A-10s continued to roll in for an hour, launching Mavericks, dropping Rockeyes, and mincing the enemy with their 30-mm cannons. At the end of it, not a tank survived; the entire enemy force was in flames. Remarked one A-10 pilot: "If people had said a year ago that I'd be fighting a night war in the A-10, I'd have laughed my head off at them."

Most of the A-10s and some F-16s operated from forward airstrips close to the Kuwaiti border rather than make the long flight back to their permanent bases for more fuel and weapons. Though the run-

ways, taxiways, and hardstands for park-
ing aircraft had been built of concrete
years earlier, other features had a
makeshift flavor. A box on stilts
served as a control tower. Fuel was im-
ported in—and dispensed from—huge rubber bladders. Diesel
generators provided electricity. One strip had a dormitory for
off-duty pilots, who bunked four to a ten-by-ten-foot room
and shared a toilet and shower down the hall. "Not your
Holiday Inn," said one flier, "but we could walk to the
bathroom in our underwear and we thought that was
pretty neat." Mostly, however, pilots, operations people, and maintenance crews took their rest, what little there was, under canvas. With each plane at
times flying three and four sorties per day, ground
crews routinely put in twelve-hour shifts. Working
like pit crews at the Indianapolis 500, a well-
coordinated team of a dozen could refuel, rearm,
and relaunch a Warthog in thirty minutes.

A Herculean Effort

Going into February, coalition air forces had mounted close to
50,000 sorties, and were averaging a monumental 2,000 sorties and
up to 5,000 tons of ordnance delivered each and every day. By com-
parison, the U.S. Air Force and Navy had flown just over 1,000
sorties and delivered 20,000 tons of ordnance during the entire elev-
en days of Operation Linebacker II against North Vietnam in 1972,
until Desert Wind the fiercest aerial bombardment in history.

The U.S. Air Force was carrying about 60 percent of the burden,
with the rest divided among the Navy, Marines, and coalition partners. Pushing their Jaguar, Tornado, and 1960s-vintage Buccaneer
fighter-bombers for all they were worth, the British alone had flown
2,500 missions. At this point, most of the strategic targets around
Baghdad and to the north had been neutralized and 80 percent of the
air war was focused on the Iraqi Republican Guard and other troops
in and around Kuwait. So ferocious was the bombing—sometimes
as many as 800 combat sorties targeted against the enemy in Kuwait
alone—that an F-16 flight leader in debrief tapped a three-

by-four-foot table and remarked: "There wasn't a piece of earth as big as this table that didn't have something hitting it."

Iraqi air defenses continued to put up a heavy volume of antiaircraft fire. Approaching a target at night, said an F-16 pilot, was like "driving down a deserted highway in the middle of West Texas at 2:00 a.m. and then suddenly coming on the biggest Fourth of July demonstration you've ever seen in your life all at once! You're watching all those missiles going by and all the triple-A going off. You can see the sparkles coming up and all of a sudden there's this big fireworks bomb burst in the air. Other times it looks like a huge red snake slinking at you and wiggling its way all over the sky."

Strike pilots, particularly in A-10s and F-16s, approached sensory overload at times. "Your mind is moving at a hundred miles an hour, trying to do everything you can do to accomplish the mission," explained a colonel in charge of an F-16 squadron. "You're in there and you're checking your gas, you're checking your altitude, you're checking your airspeed, you're looking for the triple-A, you're trying to look into your radar to see if there are other airplanes out in front of you. Then you throw your radar to look at the ground to see if you can pick up any moving targets and you lock your radar onto the target. Then you roll in, using your head-up display to see if you can acquire the target visually."

The aviator described how he selected a Maverick missile from his weapons load, used its infrared imaging system to confirm the target, and locked on, tracking the quarry until it was within range. "The whole time you're looking outside again," continued the colonel, "to make sure that the triple-A is not tracking and then over to the radar to make sure you're not going to run into another airplane and then back to the Mav to see if it's ready to launch. If it is, you hit the pickle button, then you get out of the way, back into the darkness, and watch to see if the Maverick hits. Once you see it hit, then you come off the target and call the next guy in." Finding targets for all an F-16's missiles and attacking them took about twenty-five minutes, a very long time to spend dodging bullets.

Returning from one such mission in the middle of the war, another F-16 squadron commander walked over to a pilot outside the trailer where they kept their flight gear. "The guy, who was probably my most experienced F-16 pilot, is leaning against a row of sandbags, and he's shaking like a leaf," said the colonel. "He can't talk. He can't walk. He can't do anything. He's just holding onto the sandbags and shaking. Just the fear, the excitement, the adrenalin that is gone all of a sudden. Everything finally caught up with him."

But the pilot was back in the cockpit the next night, flying another strike mission. Yet nobody ever really became inured to combat—even after Iraqi defenses had weakened to the point where at night they could only fire at the sound of aircraft engines in the blackness. The F-16s usually attracted the thickest of such flak because of their noisy, high-thrust engines. By contrast, the voice of the low-thrust engines on the A-10 was a relative whisper. Warthog pilots reported that only about one in 100 night sorties was shot at by the enemy before the missiles and bombs started exploding.

There were casualties, of course, but they were astonishingly light. The United States had been braced to lose three or four aircraft a day. Yet total combat losses through January 23 amounted to barely a dozen U.S. planes—including three F-16 Falcons and two F-15E Strike Eagles—and seven allied craft. So far, not a single A-10 had been shot down, though a number had wobbled in with damage. When one Warthog landed safely with a huge hole in its wing, the pilot leaped out and kissed the homely plane's snout.

Based on photographs from satellites and high-altitude reconnaissance aircraft, an accurate picture began to emerge of how badly the enemy had been hurt. "It's been three weeks now, and these guys have had nothing but metal on their heads," said one official. General Schwarzkopf reported on February 9 that the incessant air attacks had cost the Iraqis something like 20 percent of their entire army in Kuwait and Southern Iraq—750 of 4,200 tanks, 600 of 4,000 armored personnel carriers, 650 of 3,200 artillery pieces. No one put a number on the dead and wounded, but unofficial estimates ran to the tens of thousands. Saddam had also lost around 40,000 tons of his total ammunition stocks of 300,000 tons.

Spotting Fresh Targets among the Wrecks

And now a curious thing was happening, a development that required fresh tactics: The swarms of attacking aircraft were starting to have trouble finding things to shoot at. A campaign that pilots had first called a "turkey shoot" was becoming, in the words of one flier, "across-the-board frustration. It's turned into hunt and peck." Flights that once unloaded all their ordnance in one swoop at thickets of enemy tanks and trucks now needed three or four passes. The extra flying wasted time and put the pilots at greater risk from enemy air defenses; though diminished, they remained a considerable threat, especially during the day.

One impediment to spotting targets was that the desert had become littered with hulks; pilots had increasing difficulty in telling, from a height of 10,000 feet, which machines were dead and which might still be operational. The enemy made the task even tougher by lighting off gasoline cans on top of their T-62s and T-72s to dupe airmen into thinking that the tanks were afire. Increasingly, the clusters of revetments that pocked the desert and lined the roads held dummies. Moreover, the Iraqis constantly shifted their equip-

Minutes after an attack by French fighter-bombers, smoke shades part of a large Iraqi ammunition-storage area, subdivided by an irregular grid of sand berms. Holes made in the roofs of storage sheds by earlier raids—together with the absence of bomb craters in the sand—suggest the use of precision weapons. Dark smudges on the ground mark locations of sheds containing munitions that exploded when struck.

SMOKE SHADOW   SMOKE CLOUD   SMUDGE FROM EXPLOSION

ment around, often placing tanks in revetments that had already been bombed and blackened.

The Air Force found its solution in past experience with airborne forward air controllers during the war in Vietnam. There, the poky light aircraft flown by FACs within South Vietnam were hopelessly vulnerable to the heavier groundfire they encountered over Laos and the southern provinces of North Vietnam. The solution was to turn the slow FACs into fast FACs by giving them fleeter planes that were harder to hit.

Both the Air Force and the Marines had deployed forward air controllers to Saudi Arabia for the Gulf War. But the planes they flew—Air Force OA-10s (Warthogs designated for the FAC role) and

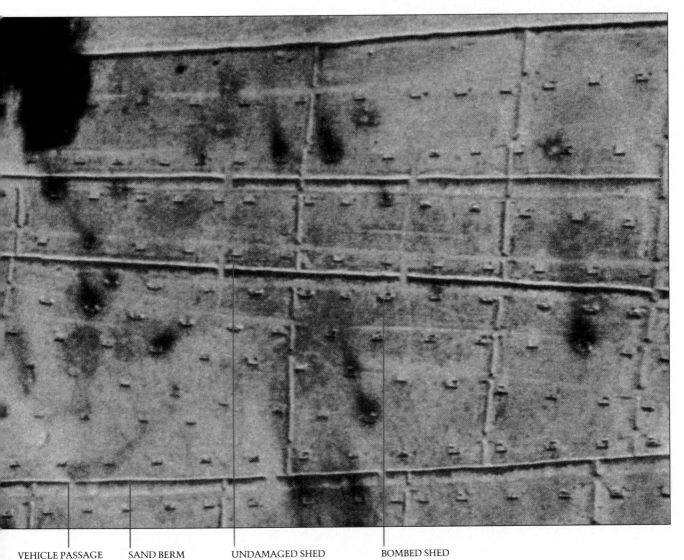

VEHICLE PASSAGE   SAND BERM   UNDAMAGED SHED   BOMBED SHED

Flaps down and afterburner
thundering, a heavily laden
F/A-18 Hornet fighter-bomber
hurtles aloft in a catapult
launch from the USS *Midway*
on the first day of the ground
war. Operating around the
clock, a carrier in the Red Sea or
the Persian Gulf could launch
140 sorties daily—or 16 percent
of the allied total, half of them
direct strikes at the Iraqi Army
in Kuwait and southern Iraq.

Marine OV-10 Broncos (lightweight, twin-engined turboprop affairs)—were intended to conduct close air support of troops in contact on the ground. They were simply too slow and too vulnerable to survive the intense flak still defending enemy positions in northern Kuwait and southern Iraq. At a tactics meeting of top aircrews held weekly in Riyadh, an F-16 pilot observed that the aerial effort to reduce Saddam's army could use a few good fast FACs. General Horner's response: Go to it.

Within days, the pilot's squadron had assigned five top-notch aviators—some with experience as FACs—to this role, and planners had marked off the desert into twenty-by-twenty-mile grids, or killing boxes. Soon the entire squadron became fast FACs, who after the war would become known officially as killer scouts.

Working in pairs—and with a tanker always on hand to refuel them—the Falcons methodically patrolled the grids for hours at a time. Mostly they remained at medium altitude (around 10,000 feet), but occasionally one Falcon would dive down to low level to check out a potential target while his partner covered him. Whenever they found a number of the enemy, they loosed a bomb or a Maverick to kill one of the targets and mark the spot for a waiting strike team of two to four F-16s or A-10s.

Looking like a child's sandbox creation, a crude Iraqi decoy tank slapped together from pipe and corrugated aluminum sits on the Kuwaiti desert. A radar reflector on a post in the sand was intended to attract the attention of raiding warplanes.

Success was immediate. On one daylight mission, a fast FAC directed a pair of F-16s to a cluster of C-shaped revetments holding eight tanks; the F-16s placed all eight of their 500-pound iron bombs inside the revetments. Scratch eight tanks—powerful testimony to the accuracy of the F-16 weapon delivery system. Laser-equipped F-15Es operating in two-ship elements on a couple of occasions killed sixteen more widely separated tanks, one for each of the Paveway bombs they carried. At one point, a fast FAC team came across a concentration of 300 tanks, APCs, and other vehicles on the move sixty miles north of the Saudi border. Attacking into the night, pilots claimed fifty-two tanks and other vehicles destroyed, along with three guns. A tremendous amount of ammunition erupted in secondary explosions. All across southern Iraq and northern Kuwait, as the enemy was decimated in one killing box, the fast FACs shifted to another to repeat the procedure.

On February 14, during the daily press briefing at coalition headquarters in Riyadh, Marine Brigadier General Richard Neal updated the battle damage assessment. Over the five preceding days, more than 1,000 enemy tanks, APCs, and artillery pieces had been destroyed, bringing Iraqi losses to approximately 30 percent of its army's equipment: 1,300 of 4,200 tanks, 800 of 3,000 armored personnel carriers, 1,100 of 3,200 artillery pieces. "No division, no brigade, no battalion is being spared attack by our pilots," said Neal.

By this time, the Republican Guard strategic reserve in southern Iraq had been so badly mauled that the focus of the air raids began to shift toward the armored divisions forming the enemy's tactical reserve in central Kuwait, forces that had to be rendered incapable of parrying coalition thrusts in the ground war that most felt lay just ahead. Between fast FACs and JSTARS, there was no haven for the Iraqis. "Basically, they can't move," said an F-16 pilot. "Every time somebody moves, we see it, and the guys are destroyed."

No longer able to shift from revetment to revetment, the Iraqi response was to hunker down, desperately hoping to save what they could of their army by burying it in the desert. Bulldozers gouged trenches deep enough to hide a tank up to its turret ring. With sandbags piled on top, tanks became mere bumps in the sand, with only the cannons protruding. Even the most practiced FACs were having trouble finding enough targets. To deal with the problem, the pilots learned to "read the bumps."

Saddam Hussein might be able to hide his tanks, but he could not keep them cool, and U.S. infrared sensors were able to spot anything that differed in temperature from its surroundings. Patrolling the desert, A-10 and F-16 pilots checked out the bumps in the relatively featureless terrain with their Maverick seekers. Some of the bumps were just bumps, but others appeared suspiciously darker than nearby sand during the day and brighter after dark. In blazing sun, the lightly covered tanks the bumps concealed stayed cooler than the desert and retained more heat after sunset. Not every tank gave itself away all the time. If a vehicle's engine had been run to charge batteries or operate radios, for example, its temperature might nearly match that of sand in the sun, but come nighttime, it would only stand out more clearly. When a pilot fired a Maverick into an unnatural-looking bump, he often triggered an inferno of detonating fuel and ammunition as a tank went to its death.

Aircrews of FLIR-equipped F-111 Aardvarks and F-15E Strike Eagles could read the bumps, too, and blast the tank-filled ones with laser-guided bombs. On the first night using the new technique, four aircraft killed nine tanks, and within a few days, sixty F-111s and F-15s were destroying as many as 200 tanks a night.

"The army down there is being slaughtered," said an Air Force intelligence officer, "and there's nothing anyone can do to help them. They aren't reacting as a national army anymore, just pockets of troops trying to defend themselves from total destruction." An Iraqi soldier, one of a growing stream of deserters, was interested only in escape. "If we had died coming over, from being shot in the back or from stepping on something and being blown up, that would have been okay, rather than another night of this."

A Climactic Four Days

In early February, General Horner had ventured a football analogy: "The score is 60-to-0, but we don't know what quarter we're in. We hope it's the fourth." In actuality, the final quarter did not begin until 4:00 a.m. on February 24, when lead elements of a force numbering more than half a million U.S. and coalition troops surged forward to begin the ground war.

By brilliant maneuver and overwhelming firepower, General Schwarzkopf's troops would defeat Saddam's Republican Guard and the remainder of his forces in barely 100 hours. Yet that army had been so severely buffeted from the air that it scarcely qualified as a fighting force. At the start of the air campaign, the goal had been to inflict 50 percent attrition on the enemy. By the time ground troops headed north into Kuwait and Iraq, after thirty-nine days and nights of bombardment, coalition air forces had destroyed 1,685 of Iraq's tanks, 925 of its APCs, and 1,485 of its guns—all told, almost 40 percent of its army. Many units were down by 50 percent, virtually without supplies or food, without radar or communications, sometimes without commanders. "The enemy," one officer said, "is blind. He can't get his orders passed. All he can do is react."

To accomplish all this had required 94,000 sorties, a staggering average of more than 100 per hour. Yet, in the next four days, air operations would surge to 160 sorties per hour, with about half of the 16,000 total flown in support of advancing ground troops. Many of them were directed from a pair of Airborne Battlefield Command and Control Center (ABCCC) modules that were slipped into the fuselages of C-130 Hercules transports modified with extra antennas and air conditioning for all the electronic equipment. Inside each forty-six-foot-long unit, a battle staff of twelve sat before consoles that displayed multicolor maps showing towns, cities, hills, beaches, and other terrain features—as well as coalition positions, AWACS and tanker orbits, and combat aircraft tracks. With this god's-eye view of the arena, the battle staff monitored communications, accepted requests for air strikes against the enemy, and coordinated responses to requests for air power from ground commanders and FACs to ensure the most potent use of available assets.

As it happened, there was remarkably little close air support in the usual sense of aircraft attacking enemy troops firing on friendlies. The battle was so fluid and the allies were moving so rapidly that the Iraqis rarely had a chance to organize a defensive stand. On one occasion, an F-15E crew was given a target just ahead of the FSCL, or Fire Support Coordination Line. Behind this line, artillery batteries and aircraft must seek permission before expending ordnance to avoid hitting coalition troops. Just as the fighter-bomber approached the target five minutes later, a controller called off the strike. In that brief time, the FSCL had moved five miles north and the erstwhile target was now being engulfed by the on-racing troops.

From the start of Operation Desert Storm, coalition commanders had taken every precaution to avoid the nightmare of "Blue on Blue" fire—allied aircraft attacking allied ground forces. But inevitably, there were tragic mistakes. In the first weeks of the war, during a skirmish around Khafji on January 30, an A-10 attempting to support a unit of embattled U.S. Marines had launched a Maverick. It remains unclear whether the pilot made a mistake or the missile's infrared seeker malfunctioned, but instead of blasting an advancing Iraqi tank, the Maverick struck a Marine Light Armored Vehicle. The LAV blew up, killing all seven Marines inside. Now, in the ground war, another A-10 strafed two British Warrior infantry fighting vehicles, killing nine soldiers. The troops apparently had removed the vehicles' vivid orange identification panels in order to get at some supplies and had neglected to replace them; in the haze, the A-10 pilot had failed to recognize the Warriors as friendly.

Given such dangers and with no great need for close air support, the commanders mainly relied on the Army's AH-64 Apache and Marine AH-1 Cobra helicopters to work with the troops. Fixed-wing aircraft were sent against enemy formations ten to twelve miles ahead of the ground forces.

Air Force F-15Es, F-111s, and B-52s; Navy and Marine A-6s, A-7s, and F/A-18s; allied Tornadoes, Jaguars, and Buccaneers; even a few venerable Kuwaiti A-4 Skyhawks that had escaped the invasion all took a hand in pounding the Iraqis. But most of the burden fell on the U.S. Air Force's nearly 400 F-16 Falcons and A-10 Warthogs, along with 50 Marine AV-8B Harrier vertical-takeoff "jump jets."

With some Iraqi units still putting up wild but heavy AAA, losses were unavoidable. Six planes went down: an F-16; a Harrier; two FACs, one in an OA-10, the other in an OV-10; and two Army OV-1 light observation craft. Flying conditions had again deteriorated. Not only had the weather turned, but the Iraqis had torched the Kuwaiti oil fields, and great billows of black smoke rolled up into the storm clouds. Although ceiling and visibility frequently neared zero, pilots often could attack by getting down on the deck to sweep in at extremely low altitude under the smoke and clouds.

So far, the Iraqi Air Force had opted to sit out the war. But no one could be sure that they would remain grounded, and squadrons of F-15Cs flew top cover over the battlefield. Looking down through breaks in the clouds and smoke, the Eagle pilots could see the A-10s and F-16s working far below against a backdrop of bursting bombs. Smoke or no, the shooters were having a field day.

The ground war—"the mother of all battles" that Saddam had forecast with such anticipation—was scarcely thirty-six hours old when a pair of A-10s entered Air Force legend with twenty-three tank kills in the course of three sorties. On the first mission, the two A-10s were called in to hit a column of thirty enemy tanks, halted earlier when other aircraft knocked off the vehicles at the head and tail. The other tanks had then scurried into revetments prepared earlier alongside the road they had been traveling.

Flying up the road, all that the A-10 pilots could see initially through the dense haze were tank tracks reaching into the desert. But it did not take long to discover that the tracks led to occupied revetments, and the Warthogs went to work. The first Maverick blew the turret clear off a tank; the pilots could see it flipping end over end through the air. Coming back around, their seven-barrel cannons sounding like gigantic zippers, the pilots hosed down the tanks with armor-piercing shells. Hulls and turrets lit up with sparks from the hits; armor plate started splashing up in a kind of molten spray; seconds later, tank after tank cooked off in orangy-black fireballs. Eight tanks were killed on that first strike.

A couple of hours later, refueled and rearmed, the A-10s left seven more tanks burning near the road, then roared on to a revetment crowded with at least ten tanks. Rolling in to attack, one of the pilots blew a tank with a Maverick, then looked back to see three gun positions open up simultaneously. Air bursts were exploding all around him, and he screamed to his wingman following behind: "Come off! Come off! There's heavy flak!" The two jinked away, later adding another eight tanks to their score for the day.

At the briefing in Riyadh next evening, General Neal described how, in a separate action, a swarm of A-10s had destroyed thirty-five tanks—and added that the crews of another fifty tanks had indicated their desire to surrender. So it went. At one juncture, a report from a forward position told of a group of sixty Iraqi soldiers who frantically tried to surrender to a pair of attacking A-10s; the Warthogs herded them southward and notified the advancing 101st Airborne Division of the circumstances before flying off. Another time, three F-16s took on six Iraqi artillery batteries that had been shelling U.S. troops at long range and left five of them blazing brightly after a hammering with 500-pound iron bombs and anti-armor Rockeyes. The capper came when JSTARS discovered an entire Iraqi armored division attempting to move forward. A cell of three B-52s, diverted from a less urgent target, halted the enemy armor in its tracks with 120 tons of bombs.

By the evening of February 25, the Iraqis were in full rout. The radar consoles on JSTARS showed masses of moving dots strung out along the roads leading north from Kuwait City to Basra, site of the Iraqi headquarters for the defense of Kuwait. Dots on the JSTARS screen only hinted at the chaos below, where retreating soldiers, laden with loot, packed themselves into and on top of every sort of conveyance, from T-72 tanks and APCs to stolen Mercedes trucks, private cars, and Volkswagen minivans. Against this sea of vehicles, coalition air forces unleashed a tempest of bombardment so relentless that it turned many a civilian stomach. Air Force Chief of Staff Merrill McPeak later called this stage of the battle the exploitation

Watching an Enemy's Every Move

On December 18, 1990, General Norman Schwarzkopf asked that the two prototypes of the Joint Surveillance and Target Attack Radar System (JSTARS) be sent to Saudi Arabia for Operation Desert Storm. In an unprecedented move, said Lieutenant General Gordon Fornell, head of the Air Force's Electronic Systems Division, we "picked up the program from deep test and placed it in a combat environment."

JSTARS operates with a sideward-looking radar antenna carried aloft in a converted Boeing 707 called an E-8A. The system functions two ways. In the wide area surveillance (WAS) mode, it can track any moving vehicle in a 2,000-square-mile area; the synthetic aperture radar (SAR) mode depicts stationary objects in such detail that operators can tell a tank from a truck.

In the Gulf War, the two modes were complementary: As a WAS radar, JSTARS could spot Iraqi convoys as soon as they began to move, while the SAR aided mission planners in targeting and assessing bomb damage. The radar could pierce overcast and the smoke from burning oil wells. Unlike photorecon aircraft, the E-8 could fly safely over friendly territory and see both the enemy's front-line troops and reserve forces deployed as far as 200 miles away.

Perhaps JSTARS's greatest benefit was providing ground commanders with immediate tactical intelligence. Radar data, besides being monitored at consoles on the E-8, was beamed to mobile ground station modules (GSMs) at upper-echelon headquarters, allowing intelligence analysts to alert coalition forces to enemy movements. The system performed flawlessly. After experiencing JSTARS, one U.S. general declared that working without it had been like being "blindfolded for twenty years."

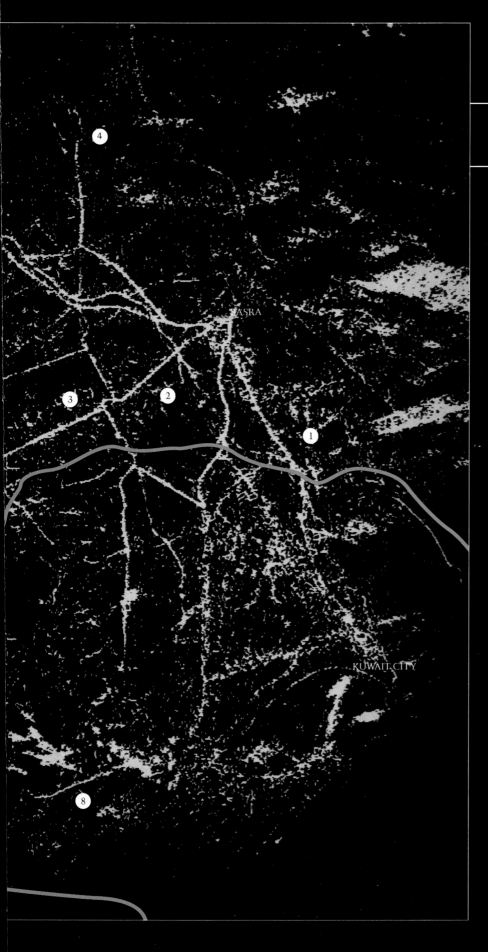

Bright radar echoes from moving Iraqi vehicles trace the road network in Kuwait and southern Iraq (borders appear in blue). The picture is a two-hour composite of data transmitted from JSTARS to a ground station, where controllers watching their scopes saw a stop-action video of Iraq's army as it converged toward Basra on the night of February 25, 1991, the turning point in the Gulf War. Some of the heaviest traffic appears on the road between Kuwait City and Basra (1) and along avenues farther west linking Republican Guard divisions (2 and 3) with the Iraqi provincial capital and points north. At a bombed-out causeway across the Euphrates River blocked by repeated bombings (4), the retreat halts abruptly. Republican Guard units fleeing west along Highway 8 encounter the U.S. 24th Infantry Division (5). The impetus for the enemy pullout can be seen in the surge of coalition forces. Lightly equipped elements of XVIII Airborne Corps (6) and the heavy armor of the U.S. VII Corps (7) surge northeastward across the Iraqi desert, while U.S. Marines and Arab forces sweep north through Kuwait (8).

phase—the point at which "the true fruits of victory are achieved from combat, when the enemy is disorganized. If we do not exploit victory, then the president should get himself some new generals."

The harvest began when fighter-bombers caught a T-55 tank as it led the main convoy toward a billboard-size portrait of Saddam Hussein on Mutlaa Ridge, some twenty miles outside Kuwait City. When the tank exploded, the road was blocked. Scores of panicky drivers veered off the pavement, only to sink their vehicles into soft sand. The rest just sat there bumper-to-bumper. No one could escape the swarms of coalition aircraft that appeared overhead; howling in to drop high explosives and cluster bombs, they wheeled around to send streams of cannon shells into the mass of vehicles.

All night and into the morning the carnage continued. At one time, so many allied planes were arcing about the target area that controllers feared midair collisions and diverted some of the attackers to secondary roads—where the same apocalyptic traffic jams came under the same terrible attack. Pilots told of wholesale hysteria, of tank columns where the lead tank was hit—and the other crews piled out of their machines to run for home on foot. Those men the pilots were under orders to spare, and so they did.

By midafternoon on the twenty-fifth, all that remained on the roads linking Kuwait City to Basra was mile after mile of burned-out hulks and charred bodies. There was nothing left to target. The air war continued unabated to the north and west, not only against the remainder of the Iraqi Army in Kuwait and southeastern Iraq, but against the remnants of Saddam's system of command and control. In another forty-eight hours, that too would be ended.

Two of the last bombs dropped in the war smashed into command bunkers buried 100 feet underground at an air base just north of Baghdad. The weapons were new, development having begun just a few days before the start of the war. At the request of the Air Force, engineers had turned discarded barrels from eight-inch artillery pieces into bombs eighteen feet long, fitted with a hardened-steel nose for penetrating power, and filled with 650 pounds of explosive. A Paveway laser-guidance system completed the bomb. On February 27, two of these 4,700-pound blockbusters were loaded onto a pair of F-111s and flown north late in the afternoon. When the first weapon plunged into its target, the only sign of success was a small puff of smoke from one of several bunker entrances. But seven seconds later, a huge secondary explosion erupted, obliterating the site. The other bomb did an equally efficient job against its bunker.

Although destroying these sites would deprive Saddam Hussein of their use in any future aggression he might plan, an unstated goal of the raid was to catch the Iraqi president in one of the bunkers. The hope was not an unreasonable one, for these command posts were among the best protected in Iraq. Saddam, however, was not there. He would survive the war, weakened militarily, but still a force to be reckoned with in the Middle East.

A few weeks later, after the Air Force had added up the statistics and commenced its analysis, Chief of Staff Merrill McPeak gave reporters at the Pentagon what he smilingly called the Mother of All Briefings. In total, said McPeak, coalition aircraft had flown an incredible 110,000 sorties and delivered 88,500 tons of ordnance, of which 6,520 tons were precision munitions—infrared-, TV-, and laser-guided bombs and missiles. In the general's view, such weapons had done the most important work. The record of the Paveway had been nothing short of phenomenal, with 90 percent of the bombs smack on target. To drive home the point, McPeak ran a video clip of an F-111 hitting a tank with the 2,000-pound version of the bomb; the tape showed the tank exploding into chunks of flying metal. As for the Mavericks, the A-10s had launched 90 percent of those missiles and they had performed magnificently. The wonderful old Warthog, McPeak had already announced, would remain in the Air Force inventory "as far as the eye can see."

Every system had functioned at or beyond specifications. McPeak singled out the F-117 stealth fighter-bomber, in squadron service for a decade. Not once during the entire war had the Iraqis tracked it on radar. "It has never been touched by bullets or SAMs or anything else. We operated for forty-three days with this aircraft completely invulnerable, so far as we know."

McPeak spoke of comparative U.S. and Iraqi aircraft losses. At the start, the Iraqi Air Force was rated the world's sixth largest with about 650 modern warplanes that gave it an impressive combat potential. Yet it had never been a factor. The allies had immediately established air superiority and then total air supremacy. In the first days of combat, thirty-five Iraqi aircraft had been shot down for no allied losses and another fifty-five had been confirmed as destroyed on the ground; no one knew how many more had been wrecked or damaged in bombed shelters. At any event, the best battleworthy planes had scooted off to Iran rather than fight.

As for allied losses, they had been minimal—only thirty-eight fixed-wing aircraft downed by groundfire, of which fourteen were Air Force; the rest belonged to the Navy, Marines, and allies. For the Air Force, the average came to one plane lost every three days. Considering the number of sorties, said McPeak, that was something "no one would ever have believed possible."

Over the next weeks, in further briefings and an Air Force White Paper, other facts came out. The amazing Warthogs, while flying only 30 percent of the strike sorties, had inflicted more than half the confirmed battle damage on the Iraqi Army; they were officially credited with no fewer than 1,000 tanks. The F-111 Aardvarks, designed as deep-strike interdiction aircraft, had flown 4,000 sorties—most of them against the Iraqi Army in the field—and had racked up 1,500 verified kills—tanks, self-propelled guns, armored personnel carriers. The B-52s tallied 1,624 missions and dropped 25,700 tons of bombs, almost 30 percent of the U.S. total. Interviews with prisoners established that the B-52s could claim much of the credit for desertion rates among Iraqis as high as 40 percent in the days leading up to the ground campaign.

The ever-present E-3 AWACS had logged an amazing 5,000 duty hours during Operations Desert Shield and Desert Wind, and the two JSTARS prototypes, arriving in early January, had flown 535 hours of surveillance without a single abort or equipment malfunction. As for the refueling effort, everyone knew that it was extraordinary. But only at the end was the full magnitude of the operation understood: 15,434 sorties and 45,955 aircraft refueled with 110 million gallons of fuel—all without mishap. Remarked one F-15 pilot, taking a bit of poetic license: "There's more fuel in the sky over Saudi than in the ground below."

The air war in the Gulf had validated U.S. air- and ground crews, U.S. technology, U.S. training, U.S. tactics. It had opened the world's eyes to the virtues of stealthy aircraft and precision-guided munitions. It proved the value, as McPeak said, "of an air force that can go any place in the world very quickly and have a tremendous destructive effect when ordered to do so by the president." Indeed, McPeak added, "my private conviction is that this is the first time in history that a field army has been defeated by air power." The Iraqis were in no position to dispute the point.   ★

The detritus of catastrophic defeat chokes a highway leading from Kuwait City to the Iraqi border town of Basra. Fleeing in every sort of vehicle, many piled high with loot, the Iraqi occupying army was hammered without mercy by swarms of fighter-bombers. After two hours, there was little left to hit. "It was," said a pilot, "like shooting fish in a barrel."

Acknowledgments

The editors of Time-Life Books thank the following for their assistance: Guy Aceto, *Air Force Magazine*, Arlington, Va.; Robert Bachman, Pentagon, Washington, D.C.; Maj. John Bingaman, Myrtle Beach AFB, S.C.; Maj. Billy Birdwell, Pentagon; Maj. Jon Boyd, 37th Tactical Fighter Wing, Las Vegas, Nev.; Susan H. Boyd, Navy Department, Washington, D.C.; Don Brannon, Boeing Aerospace, Kent, Wash.; Capt. Jack Briggs, USAF, RAF Lakenheath, England; Denise Brown, Pentagon; Lt. Col. Charles L. Buzze (Ret.), Springfield, Va.; Kenneth Carter, Pentagon; Capt. Becky Colaw, Myrtle Beach AFB; Jay Colton, New York, N.Y.; Dorothy Cross, Pentagon; Lorna Dodt, Pentagon; Leif Dunn, McDonnell Aircraft Co., Arlington, Va.; David and Tamir Eshel, Eshel-Dramit Ltd., Hod Hasharon, Israel; 1st Lt. Jennifer L. Fay, Hill AFB, Utah; Col. Art Forster, Pentagon; David Fulghum, *Aviation Week*, Washington, D.C.; Capt. Tim Gaffney, USAF, RAF Lakenheath, England; Lt. Col. Mike Gannon, Pentagon; John F. Guilmartin, Columbus, Ohio; Dr. Richard Hallion, National Air and Space Museum, Washington, D.C.; Hugh Howard, Pentagon; Maj. A. J. Jackson, Myrtle Beach AFB; Ben Jones, Pentagon; Col. Rick Kiernan, Pentagon; Kelly Kjaldgaard, Pentagon; Walt Lang, Pentagon; Rod Lenahan, Woodbridge, Va.; Col. Thomas J. Lennon, USAF, RAF Lakenheath, England; Paul Lewis, Woodbridge, Va.; Lt. Col. Jim McGuire, Pentagon; Irene Miner, Pentagon; James Minnick, Fairchild Defense, Germantown, Md.; Lyle Minter, Pentagon; Lt. Col. Jack Moffitt, Yorktown, Va.; Col. Thomas Rackley, Hill AFB; Eric Rankin, Canadian Broadcasting Corporation, Toronto, Canada; Debbie Reed, Maj. Joe Reynes, William Rosenmund, Lt. Jim Ross, Pentagon; M. Sgt. Robert Shelton, Nellis AFB, Nev.; Bettie Sprigg, Mabel Thomas, Lt. Col. Steve Titunik, Pentagon; Joby Warrick, *Air Force Times*, Springfield, Va.; Col. Mark Welsh, Hill AFB; Col. Alton C. Whitley, Nellis AFB; Lee Whitney, McDonnell Aircraft Co., Hazelwood, Mo.; Capt. Steve Williams, USAF, RAF Lakenheath, England; Ann Wood, Pentagon; Lee Woolley, Hughes Aircraft, Canoga Park, Calif.

Bibliography

BOOKS

Airborne Electronic Warfare. New York: Jane's, 1988.

Betts, Richard K., ed., *Cruise Missiles.* Washington, D.C.: Brookings Institution, 1981.

Bishop, Chris, and Ian Drury, eds., *The Encyclopedia of World Military Weapons.* New York: Crescent Books, 1988.

Bowen, Ezra, and the Editors of Time-Life Books, *Knights of the Air* (The Epic of Flight series). Alexandria, Va.: Time-Life Books, 1980.

Boyne, Col. Walter J., *Gulf War.* Lincolnwood, Ill.: Publications International, 1991.

Broughton, Jack, *Going Downtown.* New York: Crown Publishers, 1988.

Burrows, William E., *Deep Black.* New York: Random House, 1986.

Coram, Col. Delbert, et al., *Air War—Vietnam.* New York: Arno Press, 1978.

De Arcangelis, Mario, *Electronic Warfare.* Poole, Dorset: Blandford Press, 1985.

Dorr, Robert F., *Air War Hanoi.* New York: Sterling Publishing Co., 1988.

Ethell, Jeffrey, and Alfred Price, *One Day in a Long War.* New York: Random House, 1989.

Flintham, Victor, *Air Wars and Aircraft.* New York: Facts On File, 1990.

Gunston, Bill, *Modern Attack Aircraft.* New York: Prentice Hall, 1989.

Halperin, Merav, and Aharon Lapidot, *G-Suit.* Transl. by Lawrence Rifkin. Guernsey, England: Guernsey Press, 1990.

Hammel, Eric, *Khe Sanh: Siege in the Clouds.* New York: Crown Publishers, 1989.

Herr, Michael, *Dispatches.* New York: Alfred A. Knopf, 1978.

Hoffman, Mark S., ed., *The World Almanac and Book of Facts, 1991.* New York: Scripps Howard, 1990.

Israel Air Force. Hod Hasharon, Israel: Eshel-Dramit, 1981.

Jane's Air-Launched Weapons, ed. by Duncan Lennox and Arthur Rees. Alexandria, Va.: Jane's Information Group, 1990.

Jane's Strategic Weapon Systems, ed. by Duncan Lennox and Roger Loasby. Alexandria, Va.: Jane's Information Group, 1989.

Jones, J., *Stealth Technology.* Blue Ridge Summit, Pa.: Tab Books, 1989.

McKinnon, Dan, *Bullseye One Reactor.* San Diego, Calif.: House of Hits, 1987.

Marshall, Brig. Gen. S. L. A., and the Editors of American Heritage Magazine and United Press International, *Swift Sword.* New York: American Heritage, 1967.

Miller, Jay, *The General Dynamics F-16 Fighting Falcon.* Austin, Tex.: Aerofax, 1982.

Morrocco, John, and the Editors of Boston Publishing:
Rain of Fire (The Vietnam Experience series). Boston: Boston Publishing, 1985.
Thunder from Above (The Vietnam Experience series). Boston: Boston Publishing, 1984.

Mrozek, Donald J., *Air Power and the Ground War in Vietnam.* Washington, D.C.: Pergamon-Brassey's International Defense Publishers, 1988.

Nordeen, Lon O., Jr., *Air Warfare in the Missile Age.* Washington, D.C.: Smithsonian Institution Press, 1985.

Parsons, Ian, ed., *The Encyclopedia of Air Warfare.* New York: Thomas Y. Crowell, 1975.

Richardson, Doug:
An Illustrated Guide to the Techniques and Equipment of Electronic Warfare. New York: Arco, 1985.
Stealth. New York: Crown Publishers, 1989.

Richelson, Jeffrey T., *America's Secret Eyes in Space.* New York: Harper & Row, 1990.

Smith, Peter C., *Close Air Support.* New York: Crown, 1990.

Sweetman, Bill, *Stealth Aircraft.* Osceola, Wis.: Motorbooks International, 1986.

Sweetman, Bill, and James Goodall, *Lockheed F-117A.* Osceola, Wis.: Motorbooks International, 1990.

Taylor, Michael J. H., *Jane's World Combat Aircraft.* Alexandria, Va.: Jane's Information Group, 1988.

Ulanoff, Brig. Gen. Stanley M., and Lt. Col. David Eshel, *The Fighting Israeli Air Force.* New York: Arco, 1985.

The Vietnam War. New York: Crown, 1979.

Walker, Bryce, and the Editors of Time-Life Books, *Fighting Jets* (The Epic of Flight series). Alexandria, Va.: Time-Life Books, 1983.

Waters, Andrew W., *All the U.S. Air Force Airplanes, 1907-1983.* New York: Hippocrene Books, 1983.

Werrell, Kenneth P., *The Evolution of the Cruise Missile.* Maxwell Air Force Base, Ala.: Air University Press, 1985.

PERIODICALS

"Airfield Attack: Lessons of the Mideast Wars." *Defence Update,* 1982.

Air War over Vietnam. Special Issue. By the editors of *Air Combat,* 1984.

Anderson, Casey. *Air Force Times,* Jan. 14, Jan. 21, Feb. 25, 1991.

Anderson, Jack, and Dale Van Atta. *Washington Post,* Mar. 27, 1991.

Atkinson, Rick. *Washington Post,* Jan. 17, Feb. 7, Feb. 9, 1991.

Atkinson, Rick, and Dan Balz. *Washington Post,* Feb. 5, Feb. 24, 1991.

Atkinson, Rick, and David S. Broder. *Washington Post,* Jan. 17, Jan. 18, 1991.

Atkinson, Rick, and William Claiborne. *Washington Post,* Feb. 25, 1991.

Atkinson, Rick, and Barton Gellman. *Washington Post,* Jan. 31, Feb. 11, 1991.

"Attack—and Fallout." *Time,* June 22, 1981.

Bell, D. Clifford. *Military Technology,* May 1986.

Bickers, Charles. *Jane's Defence Weekly,* Feb. 1, 1991.

Bird, Julie. *Air Force Times,* Feb. 11, Feb. 18, Feb. 25, Mar. 18, 1991.

Boatman, John. *Jane's Defence Weekly,* Mar. 30, 1991.

"Bombs over Baghdad." *Newsweek,* Special Issue, 1991.

Bond, David F. *Aviation Week & Space Technology,* Mar. 5, 1990.

Boustany, Nora. *Washington Post,* Jan. 18, Jan. 19, 1991.

Branigin, William. *Washington Post,* Feb. 19, 1991.

Browne, Malcolm W. *New York Times,* May 14, 1991.

Burgess, John. *Washington Post,* Jan. 19, 1991.

Church, George J. *Time,* Apr. 28, 1986; Feb. 11, 1991.

Claiborne, William, and Caryle Murphy. *Washington Post,* Mar. 2, 1991.

Clarity, James F. *New York Times,* Jan. 17, 1991.

Cody, Edward, and Barton Gellman. *Washington Post,* Feb. 10, 1991.

Cordesman, Anthony H. *Armed Forces Journal International,* June 1991.

Covault, Craig. *Aviation Week & Space Technology,* Feb. 4, 1991.

Coyne, James P. *Air Force Magazine,* June 1985.

Dane, Abe. *Popular Mechanics,* July 1990.

Danesch, Mostafa. *Stern,* Jan. 24, 1991.

"The Dangerous Dinosaur." *Time,* Jan. 28, 1991.

"Dodging Friendly Fire." *Time,* Feb. 18, 1991.

Dornheim, Michael A. *Aviation Week & Space Technology,* Apr. 9, 1990; Apr. 8, Apr. 22, 1991.

Dugan, Gen. Michael. *U.S. News & World Report,* Feb. 11, 1991.

"Eerie Silence, Then Came the Storm." *Stars and Stripes,* Jan. 18, 1991.

Ellis, William S. *National Geographic,* Jan. 1985.

Ewing, Lee. *Air Force Times,* Feb. 18, 1991.

Fawcette, James. *Microwave Systems News,* Sept. 1, 1977.

Fialka, John J. *Wall Street Journal,* Mar. 29, 1991.

"'Filtering' Helped Top Military Leaders Get Proper Intelligence Information." *Aviation Week & Space Technology,* Apr. 22, 1991.

Fisher, Marc. *Washington Post,* Jan. 24, 1991.

Frankel, Glenn. *Aviation Week & Space Technology,* Feb. 4, 1991.

Frankel, Glenn. *Washington Post,* Jan. 18, Jan. 21, Mar. 8, 1991.

Fulghum, David A. *Aviation Week & Space Technology,* Aug. 29, 1990; Jan. 21, Feb. 4, Feb. 11, Feb. 18, May 6, May 13, May 20, 1991.

Grier, Peter. *Christian Science Monitor,* Mar. 27, 1991.

Grier, Peter. "Tomahawk: Flying High." *Military Logistics Forum,* Nov./Dec. 1987.

Gugliotta, Guy. *Washington Post,* Jan. 18, Jan. 30, Feb. 3, Feb. 6, 1991.

Gugliotta, Guy, and Molly Moore. *Washington Post,* Jan. 22, Jan. 23, 1991.

Gugliotta, Guy, and Caryle Murphy. *Washington Post,* Jan. 17, 1991.

Hackworth, Col. David H. *Newsweek,* Feb. 11, 1991.

Haystead, John. *Defense Electronics,* July 1990.

Hewish, Mark. *International Defense Review,* Dec. 1983.

Hughes, David. *Aviation Week & Space Technology,* Feb. 4, Feb. 11, 1991.

"Iraqi Gunners Fire in 'Boxes' to Maintain Air Defense." *Aviation Week & Space Technology,* Jan. 28, 1991.

"Iraqi MiG-29 Shot Down Partner Aircraft, then Crashed in Early Desert Storm Mission." *Aviation Week & Space Technology,* Feb. 18, 1991.

"Iraqi Units Called Vulnerable to Land Attack." *Washington Post,* Feb. 15, 1991.

"Iraq's Superbase Programme." *Jane's Defence Weekly,* Feb. 2, 1991.

"Iron Bombs Used in Iraq Attack." *Aviation Week & Space Technology,* June 15, 1981.

Jackson, Paul. *Air Forces Monthly,* Mar. 1991.

Kandebo, Stanley W. *Aviation Week & Space Technology,* Jan. 21, 1991.

Kemp, Ian. *Jane's Defence Weekly,* Mar. 9, 1991.

Klass, Philip J. *Aviation Week & Space Technology,* Feb. 25, 1974; Nov. 6, 1989.

Klass, Philip J. *High Technology,* Aug. 1986.

Kolcum, Edward H. *Aviation Week & Space Technology,* Jan. 14, Mar. 11, 1991.

Kurtz, Howard. *Washington Post,* Jan. 17, 1991.

Lamb, David. *Washington Post,* Feb. 20, 1991.

Lederer, Edith M. *Air Force Times,* Feb. 25, 1991.

Lenorovitz, Jeffrey M. *Aviation Week & Space Technology,* Jan. 28, Feb. 4, Feb. 18, Feb. 25, Mar. 4, Mar. 11, Apr. 22, 1991.

Lippman, Thomas W. *Washington Post,* Jan. 22, 1991.

McManus, Doyle, and John M. Broder. *Los Angeles Times,* Jan. 17, 1991.

Mann, Paul. *Aviation Week & Space Technology,* Mar. 4, 1991.

"Massive Resupply Narrows Israeli Margin." *Aviation Week & Space Technology,* June 19, 1967.

Mathews, Tom. *Newsweek,* Mar. 18, 1991.

Matthews, William. *Navy Times,* Jan. 26, 1991.

Moore, Molly. *Washington Post,* Jan. 19, Jan. 25, Jan. 27, Jan. 30, Feb. 7, 1991.

Moore, Molly, and Guy Gugliotta. *Washington Post,* Jan. 22, Feb. 8, 1991.

Morrocco, John D. *Aviation Week & Space Technology,* Jan. 21, Feb. 18, Feb. 25, Apr. 22, 1991.

Munro, Neil. *Army Times,* Feb. 4, 1991.

Munro, Neil. *Defense News,* Apr. 15, 1991.

Nash, Trevor. *Military Technology,* Feb. 1991.

Nelan, Bruce W. *Time,* Feb. 25, 1991.

North, David M. *Aviation Week & Space Technology,* Feb. 4, 1991.

O'Leary, Michael. *Air Combat,* Oct. 1990; June 1991.

Pasztor, Andy, and Walter S. Mossberg. *Wall Street Journal,* Jan. 17, 1991.

Philpott, Tom. *Navy Times*, Jan. 28, 1991.

Randal, Jonathan C. *Washington Post*, Jan. 19, 1991.

Record, Jeffrey. *Armed Forces Journal International*, Apr. 1991.

Renton, Alex. *The Independent* (London), May 24, 1991.

Richard, Randall. *Washington Post*, Feb. 27, 1991.

"Saddam 'May Be Sitting It Out.' " *Jane's Defence Weekly*, Feb. 2, 1991.

"Saudi Tornadoes Fly Most Attack Missions at Night." *Aviation Week & Space Technology*, Jan. 28, 1991.

Schmitt, Eric, and Michael R. Gordon. *New York Times*, Mar. 9, Mar. 24, 1991.

Schwartz, John, et al. *Newsweek*, Feb. 18, 1991.

Scott, William B. *Aviation Week & Space Technology*, Apr. 30, 1990; Jan. 28, Feb. 25, Mar. 4, 1991.

Shifrin, Carole A. *Aviation Week & Space Technology*, Apr. 22, 1991.

Simpson, John. *Harper's*, Apr. 1991.

"SLAMs Hit Iraqi Target in First Combat Firing." *Aviation Week & Space Technology*, Jan. 28, 1991.

Smith, Bruce A. *Aviation Week & Space Technology*, Apr. 22, 1991.

Smith, Harry B. *Signal*, July 1986.

Smith, R. Jeffrey. *Washington Post*, Jan. 23, Jan. 27, Feb. 4, Feb. 27, Mar. 18, 1991.

Smith, R. Jeffrey, and William Booth. *Washington Post*, Jan. 16, 1991.

"Soviet Peace Plan Weighed as Gulf Ground War Looms." *Aviation Week & Space Technology*, Feb. 25, 1991.

"Spacecraft Played Vital Role in Gulf War Victory." *Aviation Week & Space Technology*, Apr. 22, 1991.

"SSNs Launch Tomahawks." *Jane's Defence Weekly*, Feb. 2, 1991.

Starr, Barbara. *Jane's Defence Weekly*, Jan. 26, Feb. 23, Mar. 30, 1991.

"Stealth!" *Airman*, May 1990.

Steigman, David S. *Navy Times*, June 3, 1991.

Steigman, David, and Marc Zolton. *Navy Times*, Jan. 28, 1991.

"Submarine Missions Detailed." *Jane's Defence Weekly*, Apr. 6, 1991.

"Success from the Air." *Jane's Defence Weekly*, Apr. 6, 1991.

"Suddenly, All Eyes Are on Stealth." *Business Week*, Mar. 25, 1991.

Sweetman, Bill. *Jane's Defence Weekly*, Jan. 26, Feb. 9, Feb. 23, Mar. 9, Mar. 30, 1991.

"Systems That Won the War." *Jane's Defence Weekly*, Apr. 6, 1991.

"Tactical Airlift Forces Ready to Support Ground Offensive." *Aviation Week & Space Technology*, Feb. 11, 1991.

Talbott, Strobe. *Time*, Mar. 11, 1991.

"A Textbook Victory." *Newsweek*, Mar. 11, 1991.

"Tomahawk Scores 80% in Gulf." *Navy Times*, Apr. 29, 1991.

Tracey, Gene D. *Asian Defence Journal*, Nov. 1990.

Tsipis, Kosta. *Scientific American*, Feb. 1977.

"Two Joint-STARS Aircraft to Support Allied Operations in Persian Gulf Region." *Aviation Week & Space Technology*, Jan. 14, 1991.

"United Kingdom Takes Key Role in Attacks Against Iraqi Targets." *Aviation Week & Space Technology*, Feb. 18, 1991.

"USAF Refuels B-52s from French Bases." *Jane's Defence Weekly*, Mar. 2, 1991.

"U.S. Close Air Support Teams to Aid Arab Coalition Forces." *Aviation Week & Space Technology*, Feb. 18, 1991.

"U.S. Demonstrates Advanced Weapons Technology in Libya." *Aviation Week & Space Technology*, Apr. 21, 1986.

"U.S. Raids in Kuwait Increase; POWs Taken." *Washington Post*, Feb. 21, 1991.

Viorst, Milton. *The New Yorker*, Oct. 12, 1987.

Walsh, James. *Time*, Feb. 4, 1991.

Warrick, Joby. *Air Force Times*, Feb. 11, Feb. 18, Feb. 25, Mar. 11, Apr. 22, 1991.

Wilson, George C., and George Lardner, Jr. *Washington Post*, Jan. 21, 1991.

Wolffe, Jim. *Navy Times*, Apr. 15, 1991.

OTHER SOURCES

"Air Force Performance in Desert Storm." White Paper. Washington, D.C.: U.S. Dept. of the Air Force, Apr. 1991.

"Army Weapons Systems Performance in Southwest Asia." Press Release. Washington, D.C.: Dept. of the Army, Mar. 13, 1991.

Conrow, E. H., G. K. Smith, and A. A. Barbour, "The Joint Cruise Missiles Project: An Acquisition History—Appendixes." Santa Monica, Calif.: Rand Corp., Aug. 1982.

"Desert Storm Chronology." Press Release. Washington, D.C.: U.S. Navy, Jan. 1991.

"The E-3 in Service Worldwide." Press Release. Seattle, Wash.: Boeing Defense & Space Group, 1991.

"Electronic Warfare." Training Manual. Baltimore, Md.: Westinghouse Electric Corporation, Sept. 1976.

"F-4G Wild Weasel." Press Release. St. Louis, Mo.: McDonnell Douglas Corporation, Apr. 24, 1991.

"F-15E." Handbook. St. Louis, Mo.: McDonnell Douglas Aircraft Co., Apr. 1989.

"Gator Mine System." Fact Sheet. Eglin AFB, Fla.: U.S. Air Force Office of Public Affairs, May 1987.

"JP233: Low-Level, Airfield-Attack Weapon System." Brochure. Ampthill, Bedfordshire, England: Hunting Engineering Ltd., 1986.

"LANTIRN." Orlando, Fla.: Martin Marietta Electronic Systems, 1989.

"Maverick." Fact Sheet. Bedford, Mass.: Raytheon Missile Systems Division, Sept. 1989.

"MSS II+: Mission Support System." Brochure. Germantown, Md.: Fairchild Defense, 1991.

"Navy-Marine Corps Team—Desert Storm 1991." Press Release. Washington, D.C.: U.S. Dept. of the Navy Office of Information, spring 1991.

"Terrain Contour Matching (TERCOM) Primer." Technical Report ASD-TR-77-61. Wright-Patterson Air Force Base, Ohio: Aeronautical Systems Command, Aug. 1977.

"The United States Navy in 'Desert Shield,' 'Desert Storm.' " Booklet. Washington, D.C.: Dept. of the Navy, May 15, 1991.

U.S. Dept. of Defense News Briefings:
With Dick Cheney and Gen. Colin Powell, Jan. 17-23, 1991.
With Maj. Gen. Robert B. Johnston, Jan. 19-Feb. 2, 1991.
With Gen. Merrill McPeak, Mar. 15, 1991.
With Maj. Gen. Burton Moore, Jan. 21, 1991.
With Lt. Comdr. Greg Pepin, Jan. 24, 1991.
With Lt. Comdr. Greg Pepin and Rear Adm. Conrad C. Lautenbacher, Jan. 22, 1991.
With Gen. H. Norman Schwarzkopf, Jan. 18-27, 1991.
With Lt. Col. Mike Scott, Jan. 23-26, 1991.
With Brig. Gen. Pat Stevens IV, Jan. 29-31, 1991.
With Pete Williams, Jan. 20, 1991.
With Pete Williams, Maj. Gen. Martin L. Brandtner, and Capt. David L. Herrington, Jan. 24, 1991.
With Pete Williams, Maj. Gen. Martin Brandtner,

and Rear Adm. Mike McConnell, Jan. 26, 1991.
With Pete Williams, Lt. Gen. Thomas Kelly, and
Capt. David L. Herrington, Jan. 22-29, 1991.
With Pete Williams, Lt. Gen. Thomas Kelly, and
Rear Adm. John McConnell, Jan. 19-Feb. 1, 1991.
U.S. Dept. of Defense Pool Reports, Jan. 17-Apr. 5,
1991.

Weiner, Thomas F., ed., "Image Processing for Missile
Guidance." Bellingham, Wash.: The Society of
Photo-Optical Instrumentation Engineers, Dec.
23, 1980.
Wratten, Air Vice Marshal Bill. Evidence given to the
House of Commons Select Committee on De-
fence. Apr. 1991.

Index

Picture Credits

The sources for the illustrations that appear in this book are listed below. Credits from left to right are separated by semicolons; from top to bottom they are separated by dashes.
Cover: Randy Jolly. 6: Department of Defense, Neg. No. DO 301-SPT-91-2937. 10, 11: Noel Quidu/Gamma Liaison. 12, 13: Andy Hernandez/Sipa Press. 16, 17: Art by Stansbury, Ronsaville, Wood, Inc. 18-25: Art by Stansbury, Ronsaville, Wood, Inc., insets by Time-Life Books. 26, 27: Art by Stansbury, Ronsaville, Wood, Inc. 28: Larry Burrows for LIFE. 33: Israel Government Press Office. 34, 35: The Bettmann Archive. 36, 37: Larry Burrows for LIFE. 40, 41: U.S. Air Force. 45: U.S. Air Force. 46, 47: UPI/Bettmann. 49: Department of Defense. 50, 51: U.S. Air Force. 52, 53: U.S. Navy, courtesy National Archives, Neg. No. H28-G-1152990 (4). 58, 59: Salamander Books, London. 62, 63: Sygma. 64, 65: Martin Marietta, Orlando, Fla. (2)—art by Fred Holz (2). 69: James C. Goodall. 71: Photo by Eric Schulzinger and Denny Lombard, courtesy Lockheed. 72, 73: Corbin/Mach I, Inc. 74, 75: James C. Goodall. 76: Greg Mathieson/MAI/Consolidated News. 80, 81: Department of Defense/T. Sgt. Donald McMichael, Neg. No. DO302-SPT-91-532269—Dennis Brack/Black Star. 82, 83: Christopher Morris/Black Star. 85: McDonnell Douglas, Neg. No. C12-14003-39. 86, 87: Art by Steve Bauer. 88: Department of Defense. 90, 91: Department of Defense/T. Sgt. Marvin D. Lynchard, Neg. No. DO302-SPT-91-531740. 92, 93: Department of Defense, Neg. No. DO302-SPT-91-531831. 94: Maryann Deleo for Sipa Press. 96, 97: Igor Mikhalov/Agence France Presse, Paris. 99: Hunting Engineering Limited, Ampthill, Bedfordshire, England. 100, 101: Jeremy Flack/Aviation Photographs International, Swindon, Wiltshire, England. 102, 103: Fairchild De-

fense, Germantown, Md. 104: Mark Peters/Sipa Press. 107-111: Art by Paul Salmon. 112-117: Art by Paul Salmon, insets by Alias Aka. 118, 119: Art by Paul Salmon. 120: Department of Defense. 125: Gil Allen/AP/Wide World. 127: Ricardo Ferro/Florida Fotobanc/St. Petersburg Times. 132, 133: Mark Peters/Sipa Press. 134, 135: Christopher Morris/Black Star. 138, 139: Orban/Sygma. 140, 141: Ted Jackson/ New Orleans *Times Picayune*. 142: G. Bassignac, G. Saussier, L. Van Der Stockt/Gamma Liaison. 148, 149: Department of Defense. 153: Dennis Brack/ Black Star.

TIME ®
LIFE
BOOKS

Time-Life Books
is a division of Time Life Inc.,
a wholly owned subsidiary of
THE TIME INC. BOOK COMPANY

TIME-LIFE BOOKS

MANAGING EDITOR: Thomas H. Flaherty
Director of Editorial Resources: Elise D. Ritter-Clough
Director of Photography and Research:
John Conrad Weiser
Editorial Board: Dale M. Brown, Roberta Conlan, Laura Foreman, Lee Hassig, Jim Hicks, Blaine Marshall, Rita Thievon Mullin, Henry Woodhead

PUBLISHER: Joseph J. Ward

Associate Publisher: Ann M. Mirabito
Editorial Director: Russell B. Adams, Jr.
Marketing Director: Anne C. Everhart
Director of Design: Louis Klein
Production Manager: Prudence G. Harris
Supervisor of Quality Control: James King

Editorial Operations
Production: Celia Beattie
Library: Louise D. Forstall
Computer Composition: Deborah G. Tait (Manager), Monika D. Thayer, Janet Barnes Syring, Lillian Daniels

Correspondents: Elisabeth Kraemer-Singh (Bonn); Christine Hinze (London); Christina Lieberman (New York); Maria Vincenza Aloisi (Paris); Ann Natanson (Rome). Valuable assistance was also provided by Elizabeth Brown, Katheryn White (New York), Angelika Lemmer (Bonn), Marlin Levin and Jean Max (Jerusalem), Nihal Tamraz (Cairo), Ann Wise (Rome).

THE NEW FACE OF WAR

SERIES EDITOR: Lee Hassig
Series Administrator: Judith W. Shanks

Editorial Staff for *Air Strike*
Art Director: Christopher M. Register
Picture Editor: Charlotte Marine Fullerton
Text Editor: Stephen G. Hyslop
Senior Writer: James M. Lynch
Associate Editors/Research: Patti H. Cass, Robin Currie, Susan M. Klemens, Mark G. Lazen
Writer: Charles J. Hagner
Assistant Editors/Research: Dan Kulpinski, Jennifer L. Pearce, Mark Rogers
Assistant Art Directors: Brook Mowrey, Sue Ellen Pratt
Senior Copy Coordinators: Elizabeth Graham (principal), Anthony K. Pordes
Picture Coordinator: David Beard
Editorial Assistant: Kathleen S. Walton

Special Contributors: George Constable, George Daniels, Diane Ullius (text); Sheila K. Lenihan, Louis Plummer, Annette Scarpitta, Christine B. Soares, Joann S. Stern, Bonnie Stutski (research); Mel Ingber (index).

Library of Congress Cataloging in Publication Data
Air strike/by the editors of Time-Life Books.
    p.   cm.   (The New face of war).
  Includes bibliographical references and index.
  ISBN 0-8094-8629-6
  1. Air power. 2. Air power—United States.
  3. Persian Gulf War, 1991—Aerial operations, American.
I. Time-Life Books. II. Series.
UG630.A3828 1991
358.4′03—dc20   91-14700 CIP
ISBN 0-8094-8630-X (lib. bdg.)